Selling Used Books By Mail

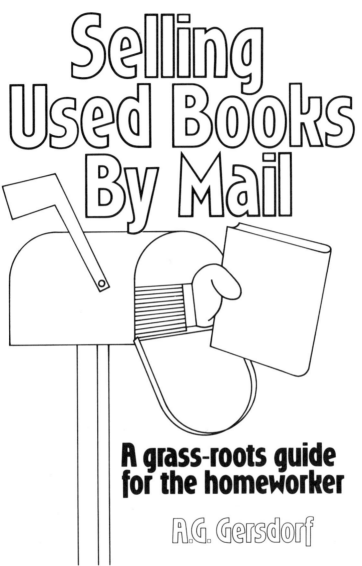

A grass-roots guide for the homeworker

A.G. Gersdorf

2nd Edition, Revised, Enlarged & Updated

Loup Garou Press, Inc.

North Fort Myers, Florida

SELLING USED BOOKS BY MAIL:
A Grass-Roots Guide
for the Homeworker
by A.G. Gersdorf

2nd Edition
Revised, Enlarged & Updated

Published by:

Loup Garou Press, Inc.

1613 Silverwood Court
North Fort Myers, Florida   33903

1-800-332-6376

Printed in the United States of America

Library of Congress Catalog #89-92249

ISBN 0-9621860-2-3

BASIC PARTS OF THE BOOK

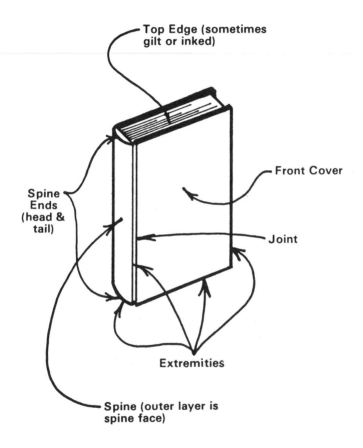

Top Edge (sometimes gilt or inked)

Front Cover

Spine Ends (head & tail)

Joint

Extremities

Spine (outer layer is spine face)

BASIC PARTS OF THE BOOK

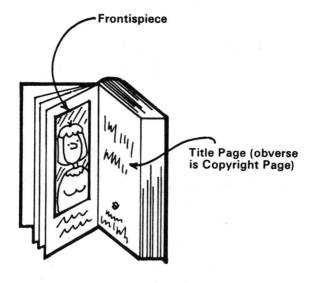

Frontispiece

Title Page (obverse
is Copyright Page)

BASIC PARTS OF THE BOOK

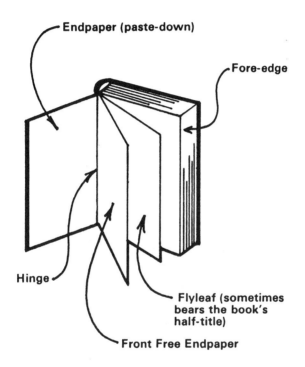

Endpaper (paste-down)

Fore-edge

Hinge

Flyleaf (sometimes bears the book's half-title)

Front Free Endpaper

PREFACE TO THE SECOND EDITION

The success of the first edition of SELLING USED BOOKS BY MAIL proved that bookdealers are made, not born.

Traditionally an apprentice bookdealer studied for many years to learn the craft. Times have changed, however, and you want to absorb the basics more quickly -- and correctly.

Thousands of bookdealers work from their homes, and the ranks are swelling every year as demand for out-of-print and collectible books increases. Selling Used Books by Mail was initially written to guide new dealers around the many pitfalls I experienced as a novice bookseller. Grateful readers struggling to learn the trade wrote to express thanks, as well as experienced dealers who wished such a guide existed when they started out.

I hope this new and improved edition will likewise find its audience.

Antoinette G. Gersdorf

TABLE OF CONTENTS

SELLING USED BOOKS BY MAIL:

A Grass-Roots Guide
for the Homeworker

INTRODUCTION

Why Sell Used Books?

This basic question has an easy answer: There are buyers for used books. All kinds of buyers, from the wealthy collector of 16th century mathematics texts to the lady down the street who combats insomnia with a good romance. Books are filled with information, entertainment, thought-provoking insights, and hours upon hours of mental pleasure and stimulation. But not all books are available at all times in all places -- obviously! Due to inventory regulations and taxation, publishers don't allow books to stay in print very long, so used ones get circulated and recirculated, _ad infinitum_.

Used books are plentiful in most parts of the country. Perhaps you have a basement or attic filled with them at this moment, a generation or more of accumulated reading material that no one has the heart to throw away. Books demand respect and we tend to hang onto them. That's not to say that their usefulness is eternal -- to us. After hoarding books for years, or inheriting someone else's hoard, a person can choose to either discard them, donate them ... or sell them to you. Is it any wonder that thousands of people have gone into the used books business? People just like you: students, housewives, retired teachers, white and blue collars alike -- anyone with a little extra time to devote to a real business.

Facts

* Most dealers of secondhand books work from their homes.

* Most sell books part-time or as a second career.

* Most are self-taught, and they make a lot of mistakes at first that cost time, customers and money.

   This book will help you get over those initial humps by stating accepted practices, showing both sides of unsettled controversies, and steering you in the right direction to learn more as you decide exactly what kind of business you want to set up, and to what degree you plan to carry it.

What This Book Will Not Tell You

   Selling Used Books By Mail is a procedural manual presenting the basics of the mail order used books business. Although vital subjects will be touched on such as what makes one book valuable, another not, or how to tell a first edition from a later one, many volumes have already been written which cover these important subjects in depth and provide vital reference material. As with any new career choice, a marked degree of study is needed from the start. Get thee to the library at once and read! Many useful books are listed in the Appendix, but they are not necessarily superior to those available through your community or university library systems, or local bookshop.

Because bookselling procedures are indefinite at best, generalities are laid out here so you can adopt those techniques that best suit your daily schedule and business aptitude. Experiment! Grill other booksellers in your area to find out what works for them. Invent your own procedures. Learn as you go along ....

You are cordially welcomed to the age-old, eminently respectable, and fun world of bookdealing.

Section I

CHAPTER ONE

Do You Have What It Takes to Sell Used Books?

A TRUE APPRECIATION FOR OLD BOOKS

Respect for your product is imperative if you intend to spend your hours buying, selling, and generally surrounding yourself with books. Professional booksellers can be fanatical about the volumes they handle, and if you expect to mingle with them to your financial benefit, expect to at least tolerate their love affair with the published word.

Old-timers in the trade will tell you that a sad trend has developed in recent years. Too many newer dealers are treating their wares without the traditional respect, merely as a means to earning a profit. Modern business advances have taken much of the learned atmosphere away from bookselling. Rare is the dealer now who handwrites receipts and makes change from a cigar box under the counter. (Those who do often hide a computer in the back room for tracking inventory or producing mail order catalogs for distant customers.) That's not to say that most modern dealers lack a feeling for their product -- quite the contrary. But you'll meet dealers who seem concerned only with making a fast buck, and more than state-of-the-art machinery this attitude has shadowed the book business. (Happy to say, such dealers don't tend to stick around very long.)

PROFESSIONALISM

Bookselling is, above all, a business. The people who make little or no money tend to treat their enterprise as a hobby or weekend sideline. Some of them, quite honestly, don't care a bit about profit. They enjoy the thrill of buying and selling and occasionally uncovering a first edition treasure in someone's barn. They don't keep records, they don't have checking accounts, they don't use office equipment or read the trade papers, and their reference libraries may be nonexistent.

Don't look down your nose at such so-called "businesses." You're going to find yourself seeking out just these dealers because they often save you legwork by doing the "grubby" work of gathering books. They'll present you with thousands of worn and rag-tag books they've collected from flea markets and garage sales, and you have the luxury of browsing for a few good titles they're not even apt to recognize. They'll make some money off the deal, for course. But you'll make more.

So the first rule is this: <u>You are a professional. Act like one</u>. Even if you're in the learning process and feel green around the gills, stiffen your back and approach your business as a truly respectable entity that you control. When you stumble (and you will stumble), pick yourself up, brush yourself off, and learn from your mistakes.

From the first day you are building a reputation. Once you're known for overpricing, poor packaging, inaccurate book descriptions, sloppy catalogs, or insufficient knowledge of your product, the impression is difficult to repair. Every dealer carries a mental "gray list" of people they avoid doing business with for these and other reasons.

In the beginning it's best to be pleasant and flexible. If someone challenges your prices, hear them out. They may be right. If a package falls apart in the mail and your customer wants a refund, send the money immediately with a letter of apology and rethink your packaging procedures. Get an impartial person to look over your catalogs and tell you what kind of reaction they produce. Your first year or two will be a feeling-out process where it is best to be quiet and observant around other booksellers, and self-assured and cooperative around customers and sources of stock. In other words, act like a professional.

SHELF SPACE

Although some booksellers success-fully carry on with their stock crammed into boxes, floor to ceiling in a basement, this lack of spreadability can quickly frustrate your ambitions. Titles unseen are titles forgotten. If you sell a book and then can't find it, there's disappointment all around. You've lost a sale and discouraged a customer, tarnishing that sterling repu-tation. Additionally, boxed books can be handled too frequently as you are forever seeking the one at the bottom.

Visibility can greatly increase sales even if you restrict your business to mail order and swear never to let in the public. Someone, sometime, will ask to examine your books, be it a relative, neighbor, or a fellow dealer passing through town. There's a peculiar phenomenon when it comes to shopping from a person's home -- scarce is the visitor who doesn't make a purchase.

However crude your shelving system, try to store your stock in a clean, dry, well-lit place. Mice, insects, heat and humidity are books' worst enemies. From the beginning, treat your books with care!

A SENSE OF ORGANIZATION

Some booksellers will brag that they do great business without keeping records, but many more sales and repeat customers are yours if you know who you sold to, which books were sold, and each customer's particular field of interest. Every dealer has a corral of regular, dependable customers, and it's your job to establish one as soon as possible. Know who you're selling to so you can sell to them again.

An efficient record-keeping system is a must if you set up a search service, do quoting, pay taxes, use direct mail advertising, issue catalogs, etc. Most dealers keep a "card file" (whether on index cards or in a computer) for recording their books in stock, as well as tracking customers and their wants.

BUSINESS INSTINCT

If you weren't born with a sixth sense for sniffing out great bargains and selling them immediately for a tidy profit, then you must develop the ability. Avoid buying on impulse and don't be quick to believe people urging their treasures on you (they'll say anything to make the sale, and if you don't have the knowledge or resources to accurately evaluate a book, pass it by or get the time needed to make an intelligent purchase). As your experience grows, so will your self-confidence and business aptitude.

Can You Make Money Selling Used Books?

You won't get rich selling used books. You don't want to hear that, but it's true. If you can earn enough to support your family, you'll be one of the few successful ones, and you'll have to slave to do it. Why, then, do so many people sell used books year after year, when they could be hawking real estate or working for IBM? Ask them. You'll get the same answer every time: "I love old books."
"Hey," you're quick to reply, "I love old books, too, but I also want to make money!" The good news is you can -- if you're willing to:

* Work long hours.

* Make conservative purchases while you gain experience.

* Generate your own good luck.

8

You can't sit around waiting for good luck to hop into your lap. Time and again you'll hear stories of dealers finding rare tomes at flea markets, or realizing the dog-eared Thoreau first edition bought in a box lot at auction was annotated by Mark Twain. It happens, and it happens frequently. The secret is this: <u>Be in the right place at the right time</u>. And that's not luck. The odds will be with you if you're in a lot of places at a lot of times. With your eyes open!

Hit the auctions, library sales and flea markets. Follow up on leads passed along by friends of friends. Investigate nebulous tips and take an occasional (but not too radical) long shot. Spend every Saturday morning exploring garage sales. Take weekend trips to visit dealers within a two hundred mile radius of your home. With a sense of adventure and eternal optimism, luck will entrench itself in your camp.

Some advice: Keep yourself available. Too many dealers practice the "catch me if you can" philosophy of business. It comes with the image of being a slightly eccentric bookseller of yore. <u>Don't do it</u>. Work within reach of the telephone, and respond to those garbled messages left on your recorder. Be liberal with your business cards and answer your mail promptly, even when it seems a waste of time. Your reward for diligence could be a particularly juicy estate sale (since you were the only person who returned that strange lady's call), or helping a collector dissolve his

library (you were willing to drive to
his secluded home).

Perhaps the thought of so much
physical running around is discouraging. If you're a senior, handicapped,
or have little time for such activi-
ties, you can still become a successful
bookdealer. Most of the buying and
selling of books in this country is
done through the mails. Book auctions
by mail are big business. The weight
of dealer catalogs and book quotes can
topple your mailbox on any given day.

But there are serious disadvantages
to having business come to you:

* You'll gain experience much more
slowly.

* You'll pay more for the books you
stock.

* You'll find yourself on the losing
end of bad deals when you can't see the
books until after they're purchased.

* You'll miss out on many opportunities
that have to be met in person.

Many people with books to sell are
willing to bring them to you to
evaluate and make an offer, but if the
books are not of good quality or
readily salable (and most will be one
or the other), it's more difficult to
say no and send them on their way. If
the seller is not a dealer, it's best
to go to his (or more often her) home.
If the seller is a dealer, you have the
advantage if the negotiation takes
place on your turf. (He's much more
likely to sell at a lower price rather

than cart all the books back to the shop and reshelve them).

The best way to hear opportunity knocking is to pound on many, many doors. With time, you may find you don't have to run around as much, as word of your expertise gets out and more people come directly to you. Experience will also teach you that some efforts are not profitable enough to warrant the expense of time and energy. If a year of garage sales uncovers very little, then by all means don't bother. If the small towns in your area prove unfruitful, then save your money to make one or two excursions each year to the city to do a book circuit tour. As with most businesses, there are no hard and fast rules showing which procedures will always work, or never work. Much depends on the types of books you seek and where you live.

CHAPTER TWO

Home vs Shop

Ah, the charm of the secondhand bookshop! Is there anything quite like it? An old brick-faced building, the smell of musty leather, dim lights and disorganization, overlorded by a wiry man peering through spectacles with bemused tolerance ....

There aren't many left, and that's not all bad. Your typical dealer now works from his or her home, and knows better than to shove dusty books into any cubbyhole they happen to fit. And the cost of that brick-faced building ain't what it used to be.

Before you rush into signing a lease on a shop, consider the rule-of-thumb that <u>walk-in customers must pay the rent</u>. If <u>all</u> your overhead expenses cannot be covered by the profits made on walk-in buyers (mail order profits go into your pocket) -- then what's the point of maintaining a shop? Most shopowners also sell books by mail order. In fact, you might find the bulk of their business going through the post office, not the front door.

As with any business, a bookshop is only as good as its location. To draw customers, you must be placed where customers are likely to be (at least until you've made yourself so indispensable that buyers seek you out). But work at home and your focal point becomes the mailbox.

Owning a bookshop can, of course, be fun and profitable, and it gives one a real "air" of a serious business. But

the commitment necessary to run a shop
must also be weighed. Regular hours
are a must, despite the number of
dealers (shame on them!) who keep a
cardboard sign more or less permanently
tacked to the door showing a phone
number and demanding an appointment.
The huge majority of customers won't
bother. Location can also dictate the
hours you're open. Big city shops
often open early and close late (one
Chicago shop stays open until mid-
night). Shops in tourist areas sometimes close during off seasons, or
limit their hours to the weekends. Few
bookshops open before ten in the
morning.

You have to be a people-person to
enjoy running a shop because you'll
eventually see every form of weirdness
in human form. You may also have long
stretches of time on your hands during
slow periods. If you have nobody to
cover for you, you're not as free to
dash off to sales and auctions. It's
no wonder that many dealers who launch
shops eventually sell them and continue
their businesses from the homes.

If you are new to bookselling, be
patient before investing in a shop.
Even a retail background doesn't
prepare you for this trade's idiosyn-
crasies (but it helps!).

A mail order bookstore from your
home will become a family affair, like
it or not. Your mate's willingness to
help with your new venture can make the
experience more than financially
rewarding. Together you can build
shelves, attend sales, wrap packages,
and share at least the physical side of
bookselling. You're really blessed if

your mate gladly pitches in with the research, inventory, and sales half of the business.

Whatever his or her temperament, be sure your mate won't resent the books taking up wall space or monopolizing every corner of the house as piles of boxes seek storage space, waiting to be organized and shelved. If you have small children, special precautions are needed to protect your stock. (My two-year-old emptied a watering can into a box of books newly arrived from auction. Served me right for storing them in the plant room.)

The convenience of maintaining your business in the home is obvious. Housewives can fill orders and write ads while watching small children. Retired people needn't concern them-selves with traveling to and from work. Weekend booksellers won't miss the football season.

The disadvantages are: Limited space, numerous interruptions, inabi-lity to serve the public or hang a sign in your yard (depending on where you live and local zoning ordinances), inability to secure MasterCard/Visa services for your customers (depending, again, on where you live and the rules of your regional banking system), lack of room to grow should you someday hire employees to do packaging, inventory, etc., and the tendency other people will have of saying annoying things like, "What an interesting hobby!"

Advantages, however, are many: Tax write-off of expenses for that percent-age of your home devoted strictly to business (see current tax laws for limitations), the fun of working in

your pajamas or cataloging books while
watching David Letterman, the satisfaction of seeing your neighbors clear
snow from their windshields while you
linger over the trade papers with a mug
of hot coffee, and the enormous savings
you'll reap by limiting your overhead.

You've read how many businesses are,
with the help of modern technology,
allowing some of their employees to
work at home. To be trite, it's the
wave of the future, and no longer considered unusual. It's also not unusual
to find "househusbands" (a misnomer)
who watch the kids while running home-
based book businesses, leaving their
wives free to drive off to work each
day.

Specialize or No?

If you live for sports, eat and
drink sports, and the only thing you
know about Hemingway is that he killed
himself -- perhaps you should consider
specializing. If you belong to four
quilting clubs, teach quilting at the
local night school, would rather quilt
than make love, and all you remember
about Steinbeck is something to do with
grapes -- specialize!

Bookselling can be easier if you do
specialize. Right away you narrow down
your sources of buying and selling,
you'll develop a closer rapport with
your customers and, with care, establish a reputation as a knowledgeable
dealer in a particular field so that
buyers come looking for you. You will
learn your business more quickly (the

basics anyway; you may need a lifetime
to know your subject thoroughly).
Other dealers in your specialty will be
happy to give advice (but don't expect
them to share customers or resources).

The biggest advantage to being a
specialist dealer is space. An inventory of a few hundred quality volumes
may take up only one wall of shelves.
You'll pay more for your books, but
you'll also mark them up higher. You
may make more money from the sale of
one book than other dealers make from
selling fifty inexpensive books.

Few specialty dealers maintain
shops, although a few specialties such
as mystery books are broad enough that
thousands of titles are available, and
plenty of customers. Some areas of the
country have enough buyers of sporting
and fishing books to keep a store busy.
Shops selling only cookbooks do very
well in urban areas, and used children's books appeal to all sectors of
the population. You'll find, however,
that most specialties -- medicine, law
books, coins and stamps, etc. -- won't
attract enough walk-in customers to
make a shop worthwhile.

Yes, there are dealers proving this
generality wrong. Once you get some
experience, you're welcome to do so.

It takes a real love for your subject to specialize and thereby don
blinders against so many potentially
profitable books you'll find concerning
other fields, but you must avoid spread-
ing yourself (and your funds) too thin.
Make sure you are sincerely interested
in the subject or you're apt to get
bored. After a few years every title
will be a familiar one, and the thrill

of the chase is half the fun of bookselling. If your subject is too
specialized and lacks a solid customer
base, you may not attract enough
business to make a living. (You'll
find dealers who are doing quite well
with limited subjects -- orchids and
hummingbirds are two examples -- but
they don't maintain shops and it's
unlikely they're supporting families
with this income.)

Should you choose to specialize, you
are probably already familiar with
magazines dealing with your subject.
Those that accept classified advertising may be the best place to begin your
business, with ads offering cash for
books, or ads to sell the books you
have.

As a dealer of general books, you'll
be on the lookout for books you can
resell to the specialist dealers.
There's a great demand for quality
books on gardening, antiques, cooking,
dogs and sports, as well as juvenile
books (especially those with lovely
illustrations), and "how-to" books. In
recent years there has been a growing
interest in fiction, especially science
fiction, fantasy and horror -- subjects
rarely treated by "respectable" dealers
in years past, but now highly collectible and commanding incredible prices.
Books written by women are currently
popular.

Many dealers today offer sidelines
of ephemera -- postcards, posters,
magazines, prints, and other paper
memorabilia. Even paperbacks, once the
bastard children of the trade, are now
big business and not to be ignored by
serious dealers. Selling autographs is

a natural sideline, but requires a great deal of study and, for the time being, shouldn't be considered.

Another general rule: <u>Books of fiction outnumber nonfiction but nonfiction sells better</u>. It's no bargain to buy hundreds of old novels for pennies each when selling them profitably is next to impossible. It's best to pay more for nonfiction that will turn over quickly, at higher prices.

Exceptions -- aren't there always exceptions? -- include whatever modern first editions are currently hot, early juvenile fiction with color illustrations, and limited and signed volumes of mystery and detective novels, science fiction and fantasy. Each of these categories requires research to learn which books are desirable and which are best used for landfill.

Some dealers specialize right off and later spread into general areas to increase their volume of sales. Others learn the ropes as general dealers and then narrow their subjects and increase the quality of the their stock. Specialist dealers can, and justifiably so, charge more for their books.

CHAPTER THREE

Types of Used Books

"Used", "old" and "secondhand" are, at best, vague descriptions for books which aren't spanking new or possessed by their original owners. A rough breakdown might be:

RARE BOOKS

"Rare" is an overused adjective with two indistinct meanings. You'll often hear the uneducated general public say, "This first edition Faulkner is rare" when they mean "scarce" or "uncommon." A pristine copy of the Gutenberg Bible is rare. Books sold for many thousands of dollars with jeweled bindings, special illustrations, marginal annotations by famous people, or historical pasts are rare. It's easier to say what isn't rare than define what is, but another general rule is this: Don't claim to be a dealer of rare books. If even one truly "rare" book should cross your path in the next twenty-five years of bookselling, consider yourself fortunate.

"Rare" is not defined by the number of copies in existence of a particular book so much as the item's subject matter, importance and desirability. If only one copy exists of a ho-hum book, it will be of interest only to collectors of single copies of ho-hum books. But if that book was a gift from Marie Antoinette to Mary Queen of Scots, it has historical value. If the

leather cover was hand-tooled by a nine-
year-old Abe Lincoln, it's unique. If
the book is from the first printing of
the first book published in America,
it's important. If few copies exist of
a highly collected book (example: the
original imprint of <u>Alice in Wonder-
land</u>), it's desirable.

Quantity is not enough of a crite-
rion. In addition, people have to be
willing to pay through the nose for a
book before it can claim the distinc-
tion of being rare. Although this
definition is arbitrary and fuzzy, it's
accepted in the trade.

Obviously few booksellers handle
rare books, but take every opportunity
to learn from these wizards of bookdom
by reading their articles and following
the international auction market. You
may have no ambitions in this direction
-- few dealers do. Most books in this
category are lodged in institutional
collections, and comparing this elite
echelon of the business with the
everyday trade is comparing apples to
oranges, as both the products and the
customers vastly differ. Learning the
rare book business is difficult and
takes many years as an apprentice to
the masters.

SCARCE BOOKS

"Scarce" is the catch-all phrase
you'll often see in dealer catalogs to
describe unusual, but not rare, books.
Books signed by authors famous for not
signing books, books published for
private circulation by famous people,
books which survived massive burnings

or publisher recalls, and many others can be properly termed "scarce."

Realistically you are not going to turn over scarce books as a matter of course, but they do come along, more often at auction and estate sales than at flea markets. These treasures are what keep you hopping and hoping. (Regardless of what you read in some popular books about discovering valuable volumes in attics, you are not apt to find a hand-written manuscript of a previously unknown Edgar Allan Poe story in the Widow Grant's dusty trunk. But one can dream, no?)

COLLECTORS' EDITIONS

"Fine first editions", preferably in dust jackets and in great condition (and all the better if autographed) ... These are the books most dealers choose to handle, mainly because these are the books for which collectors are willing to pay a premium. They are not necessarily old or difficult to find, but you must have a sharp eye, a skill for bargaining, and a willingness to thoroughly research in order to profitably market them.

OUT-OF-PRINT BOOKS

"OP" books, although another generalization as broad (and usually synonymous with) "used" books, in the trade refers to the bulk of most dealers' stock -- good, readable books that no longer are being published but are still being sought by readers.

This might include a religious discourse from 1750 or the bestselling chiller of 1983.

Age is not necessarily a factor. Older classics are reprinted by the millions, and whereas the original editions are long gone, reading copies are available at the local mall bookstore and the titles are in print. Often the price of the new edition is high enough that customers will seek out a used copy that sells for much less.

REMAINDERS

"Remainders" -- new books sold off in bulk by publishers or distributors at massive discount -- are increasing in popularity as warehouse-style bookshops sprout up around the country. They are the walk-in version of the popular mail order remainder houses such as Publishers Central Bureau. Both provide a real service to the publisher -- who must shed slow-selling and old inventory before the taxman cometh -- and to the consumer, who can buy new books for half price or less. As a general OP dealer, you won't have occasion to deal much in remainders (although the trend is growing). As a specialist dealer, however, you'll have the experience to know which books will sell readily to your customers, and you can offer them as "new" (which they are), sometimes at full cover price.

UNDESIRABLE BOOKS ... sometimes!

   This category can include: Paperbacks, book club editions, condensed
books, bestsellers from thirty years
ago that you can't give away now,
family bibles, early reprints, textbooks, broken sets, outdated reference
books, and all books in poor condition.
   But this is not a rule.
   Paperbacks, as noted before, are
gaining respect in the used books
marketplace as more collectors are
taking them seriously. Also, one hates
to admit, prices for used hardcovers
have escalated along with everything
else, and people who want a book simply
to read are now seeking the cheaper
paperbacks.
   If you happen to live in an area
where a book sale offering paperbacks
brings out the public in droves, then
by all means don't avoid stocking them.
You might want to put up a booth at the
flea market or, if zoning ordinances
allow, set up a sale in your driveway
twice a year. You may also find that
paperback bookshops in your town will
buy your paperbacks for 25% of their
cover price, or trade them for books in
your specialty.
   Paperback prices, too, have risen.
You'll find them going for fifty cents
up to a couple dollars each in garage
sales, library sales and flea markets,
but general consumers, still locked in
the quarter-apiece mentality, won't buy
in quantity. As it's not hard to find
accumulations of paperbacks being sold
by estates or Joe Public for a dime
each, you'll have a much greater turnover if you can undercut your competi-

tors. Fifty cents apiece or three for
a dollar is reasonable, and a quarter
apiece or five for a dollar will quickly strip your shelves of slow sellers.
More popular titles and oversized paperbacks demand higher prices, obviously.
Outdated and junky books shouldn't be
offered at all unless you have the
extra space, and even then it's
arguable.

Some paperback titles are more valuable than others. You will want to
pull out any examples of early science
fiction and fantasy with lavish color
art on the covers. Early "trash"
novels are experiencing a surge in
popularity. And some authors, later
famous, had their first success in
paperback and these editions command
decent prices. Invest in a current
paperback price guide.

If your business is going to be
restricted to mail order only, you'll
be wise to skip paperbacks altogether.
Dealers you quote to will prefer purchasing hardcover editions for their
customers, even when paperbacks are
requested. (Customers are subject to
the mistaken belief that a used paperback will cost less than a used hardcover, which is correct except when
they use a search service to find it.)
"Trade paperbacks" (nonfiction) are
another story, since such books are
often issued only with soft covers.
Trade paperbacks are full-sized and
usually command as much as a hardcover
book.

BOOK CLUB EDITIONS

Book-of-the-Month Club and the
Literary Guild, among others, fill a
need. They reprint bestselling books
on cheap paper, encase them in cheap
bindings, and sell them below the
publishers' retail prices. Readers
save money, and the quantities sold are
awesome.

But these books don't last. They
are printed to be read, not to with-
stand the elements of time. And they
don't. Within a single generation
pages brown and turn brittle, the glue
dries up and pages fall out. (Compare
them to a vellum book that is four
hundred years old and still bright and
strong.)

So the rule is clear: <u>Avoid book
club editions</u>. Your customers will
usually decline a book club edition,
even when inexpensively priced. If a
book was popular enough to be reprinted
by a book club, chances are a suffi-
cient number of the better quality
"trade edition" are available.

Now the exceptions. A few times the
book clubs have scooped the trade
editions by being released first, or
simultaneous with, the first printing.
Even then the value of the book club
edition is raised only slightly. Some
specialty book clubs, most notably the
Crime Club and the Civil War Book Club,
are highly collectible when in good
condition. Not valuable, but easy to
sell when reasonably priced.

You will come across a lot of book
club editions in your search for stock,
and you may find yourself tempted by
their low prices. (They seem to breed

at flea markets and in middle class living rooms.) Unless you have an established outlet for them, stay away, no matter how cheap. Save your money and shelf space for better books.

How to Identify a Book Club Edition

If a dust jacket is present, "Book Club" will usually be printed in red or black on the lower right-hand corner of the front jacket flap. Trade editions can boast that this particular novel was a "Selection of the Book-of-the-Month Club", but don't confuse this sales pitch (printed in black at the top of the flap) with the volume being an actual book club edition.

With or without a dust jacket, the book itself should be flipped over and the lower right-hand corner of the rear cover examined. If a small dot, indented square or inked circle is present, the book is a book club edition. This dot is not always present, making identification tricky if there is no dust jacket. With experience, you'll be able to make educated guesses as to which ones probably are, simply by the cheap feel. (Again, this is not a rule. A few cheap-feeling books turn out to be valuable first editions, but generally not.)

Books published by the Literary Guild and others will sometimes say so on the title page.

Because a book club edition is often printed with the same plates used to produce the trade edition, ignore any "First Edition" statement on the copyright page. If that dot is present, it's a book club issue.

REPRINTS

Before paperbacks, before book clubs, "reprint houses" mass produced hardcover (or flexible-cover) editions of popular titles at inexpensive prices. Although most private presses and many respectable publishers are and were technically "reprint" houses, the term generally refers to the early companies printing books for general readers. The term isn't completely accurate, either, as much original fiction was produced by these companies.

This touchy subcategory will be the focus of most of your initial study as a bookdealer. With hundreds of publishing companies to recognize, you should start by learning the reprint houses. Books published within fifty years of the turn of the century will come into your life again and again because people note they're "old" and therefore must be valuable, inherited no doubt from a grandparent and not thrown away even when totally decrepit. Some of the more common publishers, among many others, were Grosset & Dunlap, A.L. Burt, Saalfield, and Dial Press. Reprint editions often reveal the original publisher on the copyright page.

Reprints are easy to spot because the pages will be brittle, browned, and the hinges tender (if not broken altogether). The books themselves are lightweight -- they feel cheap. (Sometimes a title page will state, "Cheap Edition.") Popular fiction published by these companies is rarely read today, and the books can become albatrosses on your bookshelves.

Notable exceptions are juveniles by the likes of G.A. Henty and Martha Finley, or classic favorites by Gene Stratton-Porter, Edgar Rice Burroughs and Zane Grey. Titles by these and others may be salable, but only when the books are in exceptional condition and fairly priced.

Don't waste time and postage quoting reprints to dealers unless you know they are seeking reading copies and not first or trade editions. Reprints, like book club editions, flourish at flea markets and garage sales, and are best avoided unless you're blessed with unlimited shelf space and patience.

CHAPTER FOUR

Trade Papers

Trade papers for bookdealers are the
arteries of the mail order OP books
business. They serve to measure the
ebbs and tides of trends, update news
events concerning booksellers and
collectors, writers and publishers, and
can put your name in the limelight as
soon as you're ready to advertise.

The largest trade paper, serving
thousands of booksellers, collectors
and librarians, is <u>AB Bookman's Weekly</u>
(henceforth referred to as AB). Other
weekly, monthly and quarterly papers
are available and their formats are
roughly similar, but AB is recommended
because of its sheer volume. You're
more apt to make sales through its long
lists of "Books Wanted" than through
the shorter listings of smaller circulation publications. The lesser known
trade papers are by no means inferior,
just smaller.

AB and other papers are divided as
follows:

ARTICLES, including coverage of book
fairs, book reviews, notices to the
trade, special reports, etc.

GENERAL ADVERTISING to keep you up-to-
date on book fairs, major auctions,
services of interest to the trade, the
latest publications such as reference
books and directories, and announce-
ments of new catalogs by the mainstay
booksellers.

"BOOKS FOR SALE" listed in alphabetical order by seller and open to anyone who has old books to offer. The occasional bargain is quickly snatched up, and the books listed are rarely priced low enough for you to resell profitably since the listing dealers are hoping to catch the attention of heeled collectors. (Better deals are to be found in the smaller papers, but on the whole the quality of books can also be lower.)

"BOOKS WANTED" lists thousands of titles dealers seek for their customers. Your attentions as a beginner bookseller are directed here because every time a book is listed that you have in stock, you're going to offer it at the best price you can (holding it aside for a couple weeks, after which, if no order arrives, you will offer it to the next dealer seeking a copy). Section III will explain the ins and outs of quoting.
    If you wish to have dealers contact you directly with their "wants", a few lines can be inserted under the Books Wanted section requesting "want lists" (mailed regularly by search services) and catalogs. Smaller trade papers will notice your interest and send a sample, hoping you'll subscribe.

STOLEN BOOKS are registered with AB and their descriptions publicized. Book thefts are, alas, a growing concern, and should you ever find yourself confronting a possible thief trying to sell you suspicious books, play it cool, be observant, and do your best to locate the owner.

The Appendix includes names and addresses of two publications that can help you get started. Your original outlay may seem shockingly high, but will be recovered quickly if you quote your stock frequently, neatly, and reasonably priced.

Bookseller Organizations

National and international organizations of rare book dealers have proven to be so difficult to join, with stiff requirements and high fees, that state-wide and regional organizations are growing in popularity and influence. Midwest Bookhunters (in the Chicago area) is typical, with regular luncheon meetings and annual book fairs. Bookdealers in many states have banded together to publicize their businesses, and publish yearly lists of members with descriptions of specialties and services. Look around to see if there isn't such an organization in your area.

CHAPTER FIVE

Judging the Value of Used Books

Why is one book valuable and another
not? Many books have been written on
this important subject and many more
will be, as the topic is not easily
exhausted and what's popular with
collectors today may not be tomorrow.
Here are a few basics:

First editions are usually more
valuable than later editions. These
are the first copies off the press, for
which most book collectors are willing
to pay a premium. It's been said,
accurately so, that fewer tenth editions exist than first editions, but
the fact remains that collectors like
to possess the same edition they
imagine was prized by the author. The
exceptions are books collected for
content, historical facts, geological
information, etc. In some cases the
later, revised editions are more
salable. Occasionally later editions
feature special sections or illustrations, and therefore retain their
values.
The epitome of the first edition is
a pristine copy of an author's first
book, which can be worth many times the
value of later titles. A number of
people with discrimination, foresight
and hefty budgets purchase new copies
of first books by unknown authors and
carefully preserve them, hoping that
they've discovered another Stephen
King.

<u>Reprints are worth less than the original trade editions</u>. Exceptions are where the reprint is a well-made edition by a private press, a limited edition, has wonderful illustrations, or celebrates an historical event.

<u>Dust jackets add value to a book</u>. Of especial value are those published before 1930. The values of some early important books will increase ten-fold with a nice dust jacket. You'll come across the term "dust wrapper" in dealer catalogs, a term which is highly overused, possibly because it sounds "professional." (Dust wrappers were the earliest forms of dust jackets, carrying little or no printing.) Dust wrappers issued before 1900 are partic- ularly scarce and can make a worthless book salable for the wrapper alone.

Take care of the dust jackets on your books! Don't ever repair tears and splits with ordinary transparent tape -- it will yellow, grow brittle, and devalue the jacket (and book) for a collector. A torn dust jacket is best left alone (protected with a special slipcover) or put into the hands of a professional paper restorer.

Again, customers who want reading copies won't care about the dust jacket, but the newer the book the more reasonable it is to expect the wrapper to be present. In the interest of their customers, dealers will lean toward those quotes offering books with jackets.

<u>Autographed books are worth more</u>. You will now and again come across books that have been autographed by their

authors or illustrators, or presented
by them with a nice inscription. Because autograph values vary so widely
and are also subject to market fluxua-
tions, the increase in the book's value
is not always easy to determine.
Obviously a book is more interesting
when autographed, but a worthless book
with the author's John Hancock on the
flyleaf is still pretty worthless. A
laid-in autograph (where the signature
is written on a piece of paper and
pasted into the book) increases the
book's value only a little.

If the author's books are in great
demand, it's reasonable to expect that
his or her autograph will increase the
value. Signatures by classic authors
such as John Steinbeck can easily
double the value of an important book,
but this standard doesn't apply to
unknown writers or those currently out
of favor with the fickle public.

As you build your reference library,
be sure to include a comprehensive
guide to autographs, one that shows
actual reproductions of the signatures
for comparison's sake. If you get into
stock an unusual item with the signature of a famous person, you should
consult an expert for authentication
and advice as to pricing. Some
authors, Margaret Mitchell (author of
Gone with the Wind) for one, have been
the victims of clever forgers.

Ex-library books are worth less than
uncirculated books. Contrary to
popular belief, however, "ex-lib" books
are salable but must be priced lower,
especially if the librarians took the
liberty of marking every other page

with their embossments and stamps.
You'll probably come across books that
have been rebound in "library" bindings. These appear to be industrial-
strength and will doubtlessly last
through the next war, which is their
purpose. They can make an older book
more attractive, but right away you
know that you'll have to lower the
price. (Be warned that some dealers
will not purchase ex-lib books unless
"discard" is clearly stamped, or there
is other evidence that the book was not
originally stolen.)

Condition is everything. Repeat after
me: Condition is everything. There is
no exception! Don't waste shelf space
on books that have been nibbled by ro-
dents, infested with bugs, are stained
by water, "decorated" by children,
badly warped, smoke-damaged, or ravaged
by Bowser.

No one wants these books -- particularly you!

Remember you have a reputation to
establish for selling quality books,
even if they aren't valuable. If you
distribute lists or catalogs, or run
ads in the trade papers describing your
wares (including their faults), it
takes more verbage and more money to
note broken hinges, missing endpapers,
spotting and staining -- and these very
faults devalue the books in the first
place.

Be selective in your buying. It's
better to have a stock of 300 gorgeous
volumes than 3,000 dubious ones. Pay a
little more and get those books in good
condition. You don't want a houseful
of unsalable garbage.

Damage is unavoidable in this business. There are times when you'll be tempted to buy a "wonderful" book which has its front cover detached. If your homework shows the item to be worth $100 in fine condition, the copy offered to you, however nice otherwise, is probably worth less than half without its cover being firmly attached. It will be tougher to market because covers are difficult to properly reattach. Until you have more experience as to which books might sell even with bad faults (some children's books, for example, but only the scarce ones), pass up these "bargains." Serious collectors will save their money to buy that D.H. Lawrence first edition in better shape, even if the damaged copy is priced very low.

An occasional exception is when you come across a "breaker" -- a book that is structurally worthless, but carries beautiful and marketable illustrations. You can sell the book as a breaker, or remove the illustrations and sell them separately. (This is not easy to do unless you have a shop.)

At times you will be buying books in "lots", meaning that to get the good ones you have to purchase an entire box, roomful or collection. Books in truly poor shape should be discarded. Unsalable ones can be donated to library sales or charities as tax write-offs. If the lot includes old novels or popular reading, perhaps a retirement home or hospital might appreciate receiving them. Save your precious shelf space and selling time for only those books with a realistic chance of being turned over profitably.

How to Identify First Editions

Actually the question is, how do you identify first printings and first states? There is a big difference. A publisher can be running off a first edition when someone notices broken type on page 112. The problem is corrected and the printing continues. The <u>first state</u> consists of those uncorrected copies with the broken type, but all the printed copies are still the <u>first printing of the first edition</u>.

Then let's say a typing error is found on page 14 after the first run is printed, bound and distributed. When the second <u>printing</u> is arranged, this correction is made. It can differentiate printings in cases where the publisher fails to do so. Often the later printings are made from the original plates and may be word-for-word identical with the first printing, making the judging of states of older books difficult or impossible and therefore often irrelevant.

Bindings, too, can be associated with the various printings and editions. Color changes or switching from cloth to boards can make the difference between a ten dollar book and a two hundred dollar book.

Dust jackets also evolve this way, with changes made to the author's photograph or the blurb on the flap noting any award the book has won, etc. Sometimes a mere change in the color of ink will distinguish a valuable first printing dust jacket from a later, less desirable one.

Bibliographies and some price guides
carefully describe and annotate these
"points" between the states, and it's
quite an interesting subject when
controversy is present. Outside reading is heartily recommended. As a
beginner, just be aware that these
points exist.

Fortunately for collectors and
dealers, most publishers in recent
decades identify editions and printings. Basically, these books will say
"First Edition" on the copyright page
(or even "First Printing"), or have the
same year listed on both the title and
copyright pages. Often codes are found
on the copyright page; a line of
descending numerals or letters represent potential printings. The lowest
digit indicates that particular printing. This generality doesn't always
hold, however, and you must have in
your reference library at least one
good book that specifies the procedures
used by particular publishers, past and
present.

CHAPTER SIX

Evaluating the Condition of Old Books

Memorize this chapter! If you can't
properly describe your stock to potential buyers, you risk ruining your
reputation (thereby losing money) --
and above all others this is the
beginning bookseller's primary weak-
ness. In fact, too many established
booksellers keep their evaluations
loose enough to irritate more exacting
customers. Be sure you don't.

The following scale covers the
possible ratings of a book's condition: Mint (or Pristine), Very Fine,
Fine, Very Good, Good, Fair, Poor.
Even these are hedged with the addition
of "-" or "+" (for example, "very
good+").

For succinct definitions of these
ratings, I bow to Joe Wilcox of Pisces
& Capricorn Books in Albion, Michigan
(respected specialists in the field of
fine hunting and fishing books). Mr.
Wilcox is a leader in the drive to
stabilize book descriptions in the
trade. From his catalog the following
standards are quoted:

MINT. Seldom correctly used. Means
exactly, and we mean exactly, as issued
by the publisher. Even if the book has
been inscribed by Hewitt to LaBranche,
it is no longer Mint. Dust jackets
must be present and immaculate, and
books overall virgo intacta, and
innocent as Adam and Eve ante Serpent.

VERY FINE. As Mint, but a price may be cut from the dust jacket, and may have been deflowered by actually having been read, a condition abhorred by many collectors.

FINE. <u>No visible wear</u>, but inscriptions, names, small stamps, etc., are admissible. <u>No</u> actual wear.

VERY GOOD. Beginning to look like the rest of us, but still better. Entirely intact, nothing missing, no cover fading, splotches, torn endpapers, etc.

GOOD+ Not up to Very Good but still better than Good, a bit above the average well used and read book.

GOOD. Average used condition, but, with us, intact; no missing endpapers, plates, etc.; ordinary wear, evidence of having been read and liked, sticky fingers, Scotch glass rings, underlined passages and marginalia, fading, sunning, etc.

FAIR. Shaken, missing endpapers but not plates [illustrations bound in, usually on glossy stock and printed one side only]. Text must be <u>all</u> present.

POOR. Lousy, missing pages. Rescued <u>ex post facto</u> from the Black Hole of Calcutta. Assaulted by apprentice librarians with stamps, pockets, cheap rebindings, endpapers untimely ripped, and revenge for low city budget.

READING COPY. See "Fair." Patronizing term for a book which is meant to be read until a better one appears which

won't. Good buzz phrase in the book
business. With us, all book club
editions are reading copies.

Get the picture?
Now pick up an old book and see if
it fits neatly into any of the above
categories. You'll find that rating
the book isn't as easy as it sounds.
That's because you can have a very good
copy of a book, but it sadly bears a
ripped illustration or three pages of
yellow highlighting.
These flaws must be called out.
One common fault is rubbing or
scraping to the extremities -- the
edges of the covers, and joints where
the covers meet the spine. The degree
of wear will determine the rating. You
can't call a book "fine" if there's
rubbing to the corners, but if the wear
is so minor that you need to squint at
it closely in strong light, then by all
means call out the flaw ("light rubbing
to corners") and add "otherwise fine."
If extremity wear is obvious, don't
rate it higher than "very good", and
seriously consider keeping it at "good"
unless the book is unusually bright and
otherwise attractive.
Mr. Wilcox is more conscientious
with the term "reading copy" than most
dealers. More often you'll find it
synonymous with "good" or "average used
book condition."
People who own books write their
names on the endpapers, paste in
nameplates, or scribble a presentation
before giving them as gifts. These
identifications are not always flaws,
and there is disagreement in the trade
as to whether they should always be

specified. When classified advertising
can cost a dollar per line in the trade
papers, one must cut corners and you
are not expected to describe such
markings. For lists and catalogs where
space isn't at a premium, you may as
well note ink names. The buyer may not
care whether they are present or not,
but appreciates knowing ahead of time.

When should you always call out such
writing? Any first editions you offer
that are in fine or better condition,
published by a private press or issued
in a limited edition (in other words,
books more likely to appeal to collectors) -- be fair to your customers who
may prefer their books unblemished.
Always identify names or writing on
important pages such as the title page,
frontispiece, or first page of the
text.

Older books can be victims of several names. Books published before 1900
are so commonly marked up that mention
need not be made -- their presence is
assumed.

You needn't identify names and
inscriptions in books that are in very
good condition unless they are particularly messy and an obvious flaw. Books
in good or worse shape need no mention
of writing, as your customers buy them
for content. Do note any obtrusive
underlining in the text, however.

Another point of disagreement is
whether to measure all books by the
same standards. Should that botany
book from 1803 be judged as you would a
botany book for 1975? Catch phrases
such as "very good for age" get
tiresome after awhile, and should be

saved for the exceptional copies you have to offer.

I suggest you hold to one standard for all books. Call out flaws in the 1803 book such as "hinges broken", knowing that they won't be seen as a major fault in a volume so old.

Always, always, <u>always</u>, call out:

* clippings and other papers pasted onto endpapers

* cracked and broken hinges

* cover and spine fading and staining

* torn pages, maps and plates

* crimped page corners

* missing illustrations, endpapers and flyleaves

* spotting to pages and plates

* damage done by animals, bugs, children and water

* tears to spine ends

* split joints

* underlining, highlighting and marginal notes

* title labels missing from spine or front cover; title rubbed off front cover and spine

* warped spines and bowed covers

* soiling to covers or pages (including fingerprints)

* tattered dust jackets.

You'll come across other obvious flaws that should be described. If you have a salable book in fair condition (which is unusual but not unheard of), faults are expected and can be capsulized as "generally worn, fair shape" or specify "with faults but complete, a reading copy." Listing a book "as is", meaning you won't refund for any reason, is an immediate warning to the buyer that this book has problems.

Always identify book club editions and ex-library copies. If your "ex-lib" book has only a nameplate but no pocket or permanent markings, say so. Otherwise your customer will presume the book to be defaced as only librarians can.

If you are in doubt as to the evaluation of a book -- say it falls between good and very good -- play safe with "good+" or a mere "good." No point taking the chance that the book will bounce back to you by an unhappy customer.

Dust jackets are evaluated by the same standards as the books they cover. If the jacket does not fall into the same rating as the book, you may need to specify ("very good in good dj").

Your customers have the right to expect your stock to be clean, bright and solid. The best sales pitch you have is to see that it is.

CHAPTER SEVEN

Homework, homework!
(What's a book worth?)

Researching your books can be the
most thrilling -- and tedious -- part
of bookselling. Price guides abound so
that most of the titles passing through
your hands will be listed somewhere to
give you a rough idea of value. (Cheap
reprints, book club editions, and books
extremely common or extremely rare are
usually not included.) You'll need a
jigger of salt as you go along, as many
variables affect the prices listed.
General price guides (specialty
price guides are numerous, too) are
basically divided into two groups:

Retail Prices, containing listings of
books as offered by dealers in their
catalogs. (Example: Bookman's Price
Index.) Catalogs issued by the mainstay bookshops are comprehensive and
also useful as gauges of current market
values.

Wholesale Prices, meaning the prices
brought for books at auction. The
"prices realized" from the better book
auctions are organized so you can see
what was paid for specific titles,
usually by dealers buying for resale.
(Example: American Book Prices
Current.) Specialty auction catalogs
with their prices realized are valuable
reference tools. The Appendix briefly
explains the differences between price
guides so you can decide which ones are
useful enough to own outright should

your local library not have them. The
high cost of these guides will be quickly offset if chosen and used properly.

The value of having access to price
guides cannot be emphasized enough.
With such reference books you'll make
marvelous discoveries and suffer
shattering disappointments -- learning
all the while. How can you know what
to offer or bid on a book, or how to
price it, until you know what other
copies have brought in the past?
Someday experience will let you "feel"
a book's probable worth, and close
interaction with dealers and customers
will teach you to sense market trends,
but until then you'll depend absolutely
on your price guides.

Bibliographies are another important
tool in your education as a bookseller.
More than simple publishing details, a
good bibliography will list those
"points" that can separate a first
printing from a later one, and/or other
information to help you establish
priority of the book you research.
Bibliographies are geared to a specific
subject matter (Joseph Sabin's <u>A Dic-
tionary of Books Relating to America</u>),
author or illustrator (Albert Cohn's
<u>Catalogue Raisonne</u> of works by George
Cruikshank), or publishing house.
Hundreds have been organized, and you
must be selective before filling out
your reference library, else you'll
soon go broke. (Since price guides
often give enough bibliographic information to tell you what you need to
know, you may decide to wait before
diving into bibliographies unless you
intend to specialize.)

Then What?

    Okay, so you have a book. It's in
fine condition and has a nice dust
jacket. You see that your copy is
listed in the "retail" price guides,
one at $15.00, the other at $25.00. No
auction records note your book because
it isn't valuable enough.

    If you advertise in the trade papers
and the subject of this book is in
demand, you may be able to get the
book's full value. In the beginning,
however, you'll be selling more often
to dealers, and they need room for
mark-up and profit. You may have to
price the book at $10.00 to move it
quickly, which is the name of the
game. You don't want stock gathering
dust on your shelves while you wait for
a collector to come along.

    <u>Bookdealers are the most active
buyers of mail order used books</u>. Until
you have developed a stable of monied
collectors, target the wholesale market
and get the dollar signs out of your
eyes. Section III deals with specifics
on pricing and selling your books.

BUYING USED BOOKS

You are about to embark on the
Adventure of Bookselling with all its
fun and frustrations. Compiling stock
is your first commitment to your new
business, but don't feel the need to
rush. Fill your shelves slowly and
wisely, and don't let those steps
backward be lost on you. Learn from
your mistakes. Be tight with your
investment capital. Nothing is more
depressing than having a wonderful
library offered to you when you're just
blown your bankroll at a mediocre
auction.

How Many Books Should You Stock?

This is a question you'll have to
answer yourself. How much time do you
have to devote to your new business?
How much shelf space do you have? How
much physical stamina? (Don't under-
estimate this last point. Books are
heavy!)
One prestigious California bookseller does brisk business with about
450 volumes ... 450 excellent volumes.
For the beginner with more common
titles, however, 500 is a minimum
starting point. It takes so long to
scan thousands of book titles sought by
dealers through the trade papers and
want lists that you might as well make
it worth your while by having a
respectable number of items to quote.
A stock of a thousand books is even
better if you're pretty sure you want
to seriously pursue mail order book-

selling. If you have time and space,
you'll soon have more than that. Mail
order dealers frequently shelve 10,000+
books in their homes.

The best place to start gathering
stock might be in your own neighborhood. As soon as word hits the streets
that you plan to sell used books,
friends and relatives will crawl out of
the depths with brimming boxes that
have collected dust in the attic (or
mold in the basement) for countless
years. Control your enthusiasm. These
books rarely amount to much, but the
beginning of a salable stock is
possible.

Pick and Choose

Most of the time when you're offered
a box of books you'll find yourself
faced with a box of junk. Under normal
circumstances you'll separate the ones
that are clearly salable (in good
condition or on popular subjects,
particularly nonfiction) and let the
seller discard the rest. There is one
exception, however. If you don't want
the seller to know that in the middle
of all those 20-year-old textbooks is a
lovely first edition O. Henry, your
strategy may be best served by offering
a fair price for the whole box and
carting the rest to the dump. That way
the seller won't feel cheated. (Don't
reveal much information to sellers
anyway; they invariably feel cheated no
matter how fair you've been.)

Unwanted books can be donated to
Goodwill and Salvation Army stores, old
folks' homes, library sales, etc. Some

books you don't want they won't want
either -- <u>Reader's Digest Condensed
Books</u>, old <u>National Geographic</u> magazines, outdated encyclopedias, technical manuals and school textbooks.
Discard these immediately and without
guilt.

How to Make an Offer

Different people use different
techniques for negotiation. Methods
that work for one person may not work
for another, so it's difficult to make
hard and fast rules. Obviously you're
going to do your best to be accurate
and fair, if only to keep intact your
reputation as a good business person.
Little deals and small contacts have a
way of mushrooming into important and
valuable deals in the future.
Booksellers are very individualistic
when it comes to acquiring stock. Once
you're in the field you'll hear horror
stories about tactics used by unscru-
pulous dealers, although one person's
sin is another person's <u>modus
operandi</u>. One can attend church on
Sunday morning, and that afternoon
offer a widow a pittance for her late
husband's valuable collection. If a
young man wants only thirty dollars for
a book you know to be worth hundreds,
do you educate him, or take advantage
of his ignorance? What if an exciting
book is offered to you, but you suspect
it's stolen? Ethical questions will
pop up now and again and you will have
to handle them in your own way.
Dealers argue such moralities all the

time, with no conclusions drawn. Let
your conscience be your guide.

Establishing a fair price for a book
isn't always easy and much will depend
on your rapport with the seller. Your
first consideration is profit. You
must allow for a respectable mark-up on
each and every book you buy or there's
no point to buying it. If you buy a
book for $25.00 and sell it for $30.00,
you are losing money. Your $5.00
"profit" is eaten up by the costs of
advertising, gasoline, telephone bills,
office supplies, etc. Even if you're
inclined to pay too much for a book
because you feel sorry for the seller
or sympathize with his reasons for
sacrificing the book, resist. You have
a business to run, and you must run it
profitably.

<u>Try to get at least a 100% mark-up
on your books</u>.

This is not a universal rule but
hold it as a guide. You'll find that
with inexpensive books (under ten
dollars) you'll need to get a higher
mark-up to make it worth your time and
trouble. For example, you might pay
$1.00 for a book at a flea market and
sell it for $5.00 to a friend at the
health club. But you wouldn't advertise that book in the trade papers at
$5.00, what with the cost of the ad,
packaging, postage and time to
consider.

More valuable books can net you a
nice profit with a much smaller mark-
up. You might buy a book at auction
for $100 and offer it in your catalog
for $150. Books which have a marginal
appeal should be purchased with a
minimal investment and large mark-up so

you can play with the price should an
interested party surface.

You will, of course, offer the
lowest fair price possible when books
for stock present themselves, which is
not always 50% of your intended asking
price. For instance, if a guy pulls up
to your house with his trunk filled
with rather common but salable used
books, you're not going to offer $100
because you figure the books should
collectively fetch $200. Some of them
will likely sit on your shelves a long
time. You will spend hours organizing
those books and quoting them out, plus
hours finding dealers to quote to.
Your time is worth money. You could
very fairly offer $30.00 for the lot,
and if he refuses, see if he'll let you
pick and choose a dozen of the better
ones that you figure will sell for a
total of $150 -- for the original offer
of $30.00. Don't be afraid to retreat
if he again refuses, but he probably
won't.

If, however, a woman comes to your
house with one book worth, you estimate, $200, don't let your offer exceed
common business sense when establishing
a reasonable offer. If you have a
buyer waiting for just this book, you
needn't be stingy and risk losing the
sale or ruining future sales. If your
market is less apparent and some risk
is involved, then for goodness sales
keep your offer low and stick to it.

If you are buying from the public, a
fair price is often only a third or
less of the book's price guide value.
(Always keep in mind that price guides
reflect retail prices as set by established and successful booksellers --

usually specialists or shopowners --
who have the right to charge more. You
may not be able to sell the same book
for the high prices listed.)

If you're buying from book scouts
(who do the footwork for you by combing
book sales, etc., and selling books
from their cars) you'll pay at least
half. Book scouts are valuable contacts. If you're wondering how to get
in touch with them, don't worry -- once
you're in business, they'll find you!

Collectors dissolving their
collections will generally have high
expectations as to price, but they
should also be knowledgeable about the
financial ups and downs of reselling,
and they'll be a font of knowledge
about the books themselves. When
buying collections, remember that an
impressive collection will sell as a
unit for more money than the total of
the value of the individual books.

Don't make an offer on a book you
haven't evaluated. You will continu-
ally come across old books that look
like they should be valuable -- quality
bindings, lots of photo plates -- but
aren't because their subjects aren't
interesting, or the book was originally
printed in great quantity. Should you
have doubts about a particular book,
jot down the bibliographic information
and do your homework first. People are
generally reasonable, and they don't
want you to make an uneducated offer,
either. Half the reason they call a
dealer in the first place is to satisfy
their curiosity as to the value of
their books, and to get a higher price
than they might otherwise get.

You're not expected to know off the top of your head what thousands of old books are worth. If the seller is pushy (you'll be told over and over that someone else expressed interest and will be coming by later -- you'll recognize the gambit if you've ever bought a used car), and you can guess that book is worth at least, let's say, $75.00, then tell him, "If you want cash this moment, I'll give you $10.00. Or you can wait until tomorrow at which time I may be able to offer more." Chances are he'll wait, unless he knows for certain that the book is worthless -- you might not be the first dealer he's called.

Don't ever make an offer over the telephone for unseen merchandise unless you're working with a dealer or scout you have reason to trust. The layman can't accurately describe a book's condition because he's looking at it through a layman's eyes. What's "very good" to him (the covers aren't coming off, and the paint stains hardly show) may not even be "good" to you. Or the seller may not have the experience to recognize a book club edition or the lack of a plate.

Things to Watch Out For

"Have I got a deal for you!"
As an eager beginner, you are particularly vulnerable to a sales pitch from someone you think knows more than you do about books. Scouts and other dealers can easily pass on their slow sellers to you with very convincing pressure. You probably won't be

able to duck all the losers, but if you
get burned once or twice by the same
person, either get firmer about saying
no or back off completely.

Another common problem is the voice
on the telephone excitedly describing
her Dickens first edition, but you
realize instantly that it is published
by a reprint house -- and you have to
let them down. Or another voice will
insist that their family's 100-year-old
bible is worth a fortune, but you know
that few bibles are. Or convince
another that her 30-volume set of <u>The
Complete Works of Thackeray</u> isn't worth
the shelf space needed to house it.
(Ordinary sets of literary works are
generally valued at "a buck a book",
although this is often too much as sets
are hard to sell, expensive to ship,
and they take up too much room.)

Negotiating with the public can be
uncomfortable unless you're born with
the knack and a silvery tongue. The
people who call you are often selling
family heirlooms because they need the
money or the space, or the books once
belonged to members of the family who
have died.

Don't be afraid to admit to being a
novice. Doing so will make lots of
people eager to share what they know,
right or wrong. You should ask for
extra time to learn about a book's
history and sales record, if necessary.
You may even want to telephone other
dealers with specialized knowledge
about the book or collection offered to
you. They're generally happy to tell
what they know, or point you in the
right direction, but don't expect them
to share customers or contacts or do

your dirty work for you. And don't
make a pest of yourself, obviously.
(Getting in good with a local dealer
willing to show you the ropes could be
the best investment you make. Buy
reference books from him, or even some
stock that won't make you much money.
Think of it as tuition.)

Use common sense, and above all else
keep in mind that you are running a
business. You must be fair and ethical, and expect others to treat you
with respect even if you are a
beginner.

A warning to new dealers who live in
warm, humid climates: Buying from the
general public is especially risky
because books that have been stored in
attics and basements are susceptible to
mildew and infestation by unpleasant
varmints. If you mix those books with
your stock at home, you could end up
with a catastrophe on your hands. If a
book feels damp, has powdery covers or
smells awful, decline it outright.
Look for brownish holes and "tunnels"
in the paper and bindings, and the
skeletons of damaging critters.

Where to Buy Used Books

LOCAL ADVERTISING

Whether a formal want ad in your
town newspaper or a notice tacked up on
the community bulletin board at your
grocery store, library or post office --
ads can be a good way of getting people
to offer you their old books ... in
some areas. Metropolitan regions and

older towns are usually better suited
for a local campaign than areas filled
with young families, house trailers,
apartments or tourists.

Compare the cost of advertising to
the response produced. That three-by-
five card hanging in the library may
prove more valuable than a quarter-per-
word classified in the town crier.
Advertising can best be tested by trial
and error. If it works for you,
great. If not, try something else.

BUYING AT AUCTION

Buying stock from the public is an
inexpensive way to break your teeth as
a bookseller. You're not apt to lose
much money, and the education is
valuable. The next step up is buying
books from one or more of the many book
auction houses that are popping up all
over. With luck, you'll have one
nearby you can attend, although book
auctions usually have most of their
activity going on behind the scenes,
through the mails and over the
telephone.

Lists of auction houses are found in
the various reference books for dealers, and they advertise in the trade
papers. Catalog subscriptions are
expensive but that's an investment
you'll have to make if you want to get
involved. Once you've established
yourself as a customer, you might get
the catalogs without charge. Catalogs
-- especially the ones we all prefer,
with clear photos and lots of description -- are expensive to prepare and
mail. The price of the fancy ones can

exceed $10.00 each, but dealers hang onto them (with the list of "prices realized" distributed after the sale) as reference materials.

In the catalogs, the books are usually divided by subject matter. Each book's publishing data (names and dates on the title and copyright pages, the edition and printing, etc.) should be listed, along with a description of the book's physical condition. If the book is important, the points will be enumerated and the scarcity and history, if known, stressed. Some auction houses will say a word or two about the author or the contents of the book, even providing quotes. (While this makes interesting reading, it's not necessary from a business point of view.) Reference books that lend importance to the book will be cited, usually at the end of the description, often with the citation number.

You'll be interested in noting the "estimated value" of each book listed. This is presented in the right hand margin after each book, usually with a range such as "$20-$40." Don't swallow these figures as gospel -- double-check them yourself.

Experience will teach you which auction houses fairly estimate the books, or if the values are pumped up. The values, once again, are <u>retail</u> -- the price you can expect to get from your customers. You don't want to pay those prices at auction. Ideally, you should be able to bid half the estimated value and secure the book. A few years ago this was standard procedure, but auctions have become so popular that collectors now have invaded the

sales, and they're willing to pay
higher prices. Also auction houses
offer the best source for buying truly
fine and unusual books, which demand
higher prices.

If you have questions about a
specific item, call the auctioneer and
ask. They're only human and can accidently omit facts or make mistakes.
Remember that a book described as a
first edition isn't necessarily a first
printing (although they usually are).
If you are familiar with the distin-
guishing points, feel free to call and
find out if the points are present.
You might not want to educate the
auctioneer too much, however, as his
job is to get as much money for the
book as possible, and anything he
discovers due to your call will cer-
tainly be emphasized to the live
audience at the auction, increasing
your competition.

Very important: <u>Carefully read the
"Terms and Conditions" of each auction
house</u>.

There are no set rules as to how
auctioneers conduct business. Some
allow refunds for valid reasons (proof
of an inaccurate description or a
missing plate), others never for any
reason. Some guarantee their descriptions, most won't. Many now
require a 10% "buyer's premium",
meaning you pay your successful bid
amount plus another 10%. And don't
forget to add the fee for packaging,
shipping and insurance if you don't
live nearby. Keep these extra charges
in mind when you establish your bid
amount.

You will need to obtain the catalogs for several auction houses and compare the prices realized to the estimated values to get a feel for how each company works. Some will consistently sell at the estimated value or higher. Others are consistently lower. And because not every auction house knows everything about every book, you'll find that mistakes are made to your advantage. An auction listing mostly western and Indian books may have an oddball collection of Burns poetry that you can get for a few dollars because their regular customers aren't interested. Or the auction house can have books undervalued that are out of their specialty knowledge. Or they can gather up box lots of books on various subjects that they want to move out, regardless of value. Such occurrences make the auction game fun.

Attending an auction in person is worth a few hour's drive if need be. All gloves are off during the inspection period and bidding, but afterward camaraderie runs high. Watching the dealers bid against each other is an education. Some have secret little signals no one but the auctioneer can see. Some always hold off until the last to toss in a bid. Others seem determined to get certain books and drastically overbid to do so (a fact you should consider when using auction guides as a reference). Some dealers only bid on the cream, and the mere raising of their paddles will incite the other dealers to bid.

When inspecting books before an auction, the same rules apply as when evaluating any books. The best advice,

however, is to keep detached enough so
that you can walk away. Don't get
caught up in a bidding war. Don't bid
on books you haven't inspected, or ones
you're not sure will sell. And when
attending in person, make sure you've
read the terms and conditions as to the
auction house's policy on returns and
methods of payment. Some auction
houses will accept only cash or cash-
ier's checks. Some won't accept credit
cards. Some will only take a local
check until they know you better.
Always bring your state "resale number"
or you'll be required to pay sales tax
on your purchase.

Get to know your more fruitful
auction houses. Discover which ones
handle the books you're most anxious to
buy, and treat their customers fairly.
The more you know about individual
houses, the lower your risks in buying
through them. Buying books unseen is
always risky, especially since win or
lose you're generally stuck with them.
But auctions are a marvelous way to
find quality books, especially if you
can't or prefer not to buy from the
general public.

FLEA MARKETS

Books sold at flea markets are usually books that belong at flea markets.
They are mostly reading copies, not
fine first editions of important books.
You'll find much more fiction than nonfiction.

Books are plentiful and the prices
are right, usually a couple dollars
each for hardbacks and a buck for paper-

backs. Occasionally you'll find what
is essentially a bookstore, complete
with floor-to-ceiling shelves and
alphabetized stock. More often the
books will bulge from boxes, encrusted
with grime, shoved under tables or
between broken television sets. Too
often you can't reach them at all
without crawling through a mountain of
junk, and just as often the trouble
wasn't worth the soap it'll take to
wash up. But the hunt is one of the
adventures of bookselling!

Bring cash, and don't quibble about
paying sales tax (your resale number
may be useless). As always, come away
only with quality books and leave the
rest. You're money ahead to find
nothing than to buy books that don't
complement your stock. Feel free to
bargain; you're a fool if you don't.

LIBRARY AND CHARITY SALES

Libraries and other community
organizations such as church groups
collect donations of books and hold
sales to raise funds. The sale may be
small (a few hundred books in the
basement) or large (an outdoor sale
with huge circus tents). The people
setting up these sales usually know
little about the books they collect,
and their ambition is to move the books
out. Such sales present a wonderful
opportunity to gather stock. The books
are generally clean and displayed so
the titles are obvious. You're encouraged to handle the books. Bargaining
is possible, especially toward the end
of the sale, although you may appear to

be a cad since the affair is sponsored
by charity.

Pricing is done various way (by the
book, table or box), the most welcome
being when all hardbacks are one price
and paperbacks even less. A "Dutch
Sale" means that the prices change each
day of the sale, starting higher and
stepping down until the final day, when
books are practically given away.

Some groups are smart enough to
consult a bookdealer, who will scan the
stock before the sale and pull out the
better books. These are priced individually and placed on a separate table,
or auctioned off before the sale is
opened to the general public, often at
a party with a cover charge.
Booksellers in the area are notified
ahead of time when they can get an
advance look at the books (for a fee).
If given the opportunity, attend one of
these screenings, otherwise you have to
wait in long lines with the public, and
once the doors are opened, the competition is fierce and bloody. All's fair
in love and book-buying. There are no
friends at these sales.

Again, pay with cash (get a receipt), and you would be wise to bring
bags or boxes if you plan to buy in
quantity.

Gaining in popularity are retail
stores sponsored by groups such as
Goodwill Industries, Salvation Army,
and various charitable brotherhoods.
There you'll find a corner filled with
books, mostly of the flea market
quality only cleaner. It can pay to
make friends with the managers and pop
in often. Spread your business cards
around, and when books are donated that

look to be more valuable than usual, you'll be the first one called. The charity benefits because they know you'll pay more than the dollar each they charge for novels. You'll benefit because you'll have first crack at potentially worthwhile stock for a good price.

HOUSE AND GARAGE SALES

As a beginning bookseller, I picked up a lovely copy of a book about Lithuanian cemeteries for 13 cents (the seller set the price) and sold it immediately for $16.00. I could have charged more, but was delighted with the quick profit.

Garage sales are a fun source of stock _if_:

* you live in an urban area.

* you have time and energy for running around.

* you're choosy about the books you select.

* you're an early bird.

Garage sales are rarely a good source for quality books (people know to hang onto them). Most often you'll find tables ladened with book club editions, condensed books and paperbacks. When you do find good ones, the cautious owners might price them skyhigh. There's no reasoning with them, either. Too often you'll meet folks convinced that their Hemingway is a priceless first edition, when you know it's a worn out book club edition.

Garage sales are an entertaining way to gather stock when you're a beginning bookseller, but you may learn with experience that there are more productive ways to spend your time.

The rules are a little different when attending house and estate sales conducted by professionals. They can, in ignorance or greed, price good books at many times their real worth, based on the assumption that the dozens or hundreds of people buzzing outside the doors for hours before the sale starts are going to grab and buy indiscriminately, which is only too true. Don't fall victim to the excitement of an estate sale and pay too much. Learn which professionals routinely overprice and simply avoid their sales.

If you see that no one is buying the overpriced books that would make good stock, come back after the sale and see if some bargaining can't be done. Remember, no commission is made on unsold items.

ANTIQUE SHOPS

Antique dealers don't usually care to mess with books, which can be to your advantage because the prices should be right when you find them squirreled away in an unobtrusive corner. If the antique shops you visit have no books on display, ask about them. Perhaps the dealer chooses not to give them shelf space but has some in storage.

When antique dealers are unknowledge-
able about books, they can make the
same mistake as the general public and
overprice. There isn't much you can do
about it, especially if it's known
you're a bookseller (they can think you
want to nab their treasures for next to
nothing).

If you have antique shops in your
community and get along well with their
managers, be lavish with business cards
so you can be contacted should books
become available through estate sales
or auctions.

BOOKSHOPS

You will learn a lot about old books
by prowling around other dealers'
shops. Notice, first, how the stock is
organized -- or not organized. The
image of a dark, musty and cluttered
shop may be nostalgic, yet such a
layout could hurt profits. It's annoying to have to dig through boxes of
books that have awaited shelving for
two years (trust me, the dealers know
darn well what's in those boxes), and
poor lighting will quickly dampen your
attempts to scan spine titles. Soiled
books, too, are not inviting to
examine.

Is the stock separated by category?
Are the authors' names alphabetized?
Are expensive books shelved in a pro-
tective case so they aren't pawed by
browsers? Take mental notes to apply
to your own management of stock.

After checking out a few shops,
you'll notice some book titles are so
numerous that every dealer has one or

67

more copies. You'll avoid buying these
books yourself because very common
books aren't likely to sell well by
mail order. If a dealer receives 20
quotes for one book requested by a
customer, he's not as likely to select
yours.

Compare the prices set by these dealers. Does your research agree that
they are reasonable? Don't study those
prices with an eye for buying -- books
bought at a shop won't give you room
for mark-up. Bookshops routinely
charge more than at-home dealers, and
even if you're offered a generous 20%
dealer discount, you won't have room
for profit.

Of course there are exceptions,
which is half the fun of rummaging
through bookshops. You quite possibly
could find a "sleeper" -- a book
accidently priced too low, usually
because the seller doesn't recognize
the book's importance. You are entitled to jump on such treasures without
guilt; they're part of the game of
bookselling. You are not entitled to
rub the dealer's nose in his error
after you've made your purchase. The
best strategy is to rejoice in silence,
and follow the Golden Rule because
sooner or later you're going to be on
the short end of a similar deal.

More and more specialty bookshops
are opening, with their books concen-
trating on one subject or one genre
(mystery novels, fishing and hunting,
etc.) When these shop take in books
that are outside of their selected
subject, they'll shed them for next to
nothing -- to your advantage, if you're
in the right place at the right time.

Bookshops are usually willing to lower their prices if you buy several books at one time.

Don't ask dealers to extend credit to you. Don't ask to buy books "on approval" so you can show them to potential customers. You are welcome to ask for a discount, however, after you've identified yourself as a fellow dealer. Ten to twenty percent is standard, but not all shops offer a professional discount. Be sure to present your state resale number to avoid paying sales tax. (If you shop outside of your home state and are taking the books with you, you'll be required to pay tax anyway unless you have a resale number for that state. You can avoid the tax by having the books shipped, but there's an added cost for postage and insurance.)

Books you buy at shops are not returnable unless you can prove hidden defects, and even then the bookseller has the option of exercising <u>caveat emptor</u> and refusing. You are expected to know what you're buying. Now and then unethical dealers will hype a book until you purchase it, and later you'll realize you were duped. Consider it a learning experience, and don't plunk down a lot of money until you're sure of what you're buying.

BOOK FAIRS

Sales and exhibits put on by groups of booksellers can teach you much, but don't expect to use them as a source of stock. Dealers often hike their prices for fairs since set-up is difficult and

time-consuming, and they pay a fee to
participate. Introduce yourself around
and if you have a specialty, make it
known. Pass out those business cards!

Examine the books displayed at fairs
as you would in a bookshop. Common
books will not be shown. You'll be
free to handle valuable and thrilling
volumes, and that alone justifies the
price of admission.

Occasionally you'll meet dealers who
snub you, the beginner. Brush them
off. They'll come around when they see
how serious and professional you are.
Remember what they may have forgotten --
bookdealers don't compete with each
other, they compete only with the
market. With millions of books and
thousands of customers, there's plenty
of room in the trade for everyone
willing to work hard and keep his or
her nose clean.

CHAPTER ONE

Selling Used Books

The majority of your customers will not be collectors of pristine auto-graphed copies of William Faulkner first editions. Besides the elite collectors, you'll be selling to:

* other dealers, for their stock and specific customers.

* readers who want inexpensive or uncommon books by a particular author or on a particular subject, for content alone.

* libraries, public, private and university.

* businesses that maintain private libraries for reference.

* researchers needing information (local histories, genealogies, etc.).

* students, museums, historical societies, authors seeking copies of their own books, etc.

Pricing Your Books

There are as many pricing standards for used books as there are booksellers. You'll find one of them price a book club edition at ten dollars when everyone else has it at one dollar. You'll find another knowingly put out a nice book valued at $50.00 for only

half that, just to get rid of it. Some
will price everything well above market
and never budge. Others care only
about a quick turnover, and their
prices are rock-bottom.

Experience more than reference books
and price guides will teach you how to
evaluate a book's worth and then how to
assign your asking price. If the item
stays in stock too long, it may be overpriced. If you receive several orders
for one book, it was probably priced
too low.

The Appendix briefly examines the
worth and worthlessness of a few of the
many price guides available to booksellers, and in the beginning you'll probably depend heavily on them to determine the value of your stock. Later
you'll research only those books which
appear to have some real value, meaning
you won't waste time looking up those
you'll know are worth only a few
dollars.

Let's say you have a first edition
of an important novel. American Book
Prices Current shows that a copy sold
at auction a few years earlier, but it
was a fine copy, and inscribed by the
author to his mother. Right away you
know that this reference will not
figure in your price, and you will
disregard it.

When you look up your book in the
most recent edition of Bookman's Price
Index, you find a good copy in a worn
dust jacket listed at $100. You know
that BPI gets its listings from selected dealers' catalogs. The prices are
retail, and not necessarily the final
prices at which the books sold, if

indeed they sold at all. Now you must consider:

* Which dealer set this price? (Both BPI and ABPC code their listings so you'll know.) Is the dealer known to price fairly? Some bookshops are internationally famous, and their well-heeled customers can pay double what a book is worth.

* Does the listing mention the condition of the book? If not, it is assumed to be in "very good" shape, without a dust jacket unless one is specified.

* How has inflation or market demand affected the value of the book since the listing appeared? When celebrities or authors die, interest in their books temporarily rises. Historical anniversaries and television mini-series can create a demand for certain books, but it passes eventually. The fickle public can favor one author for awhile, and then drop him for another in the blink of an eye. Only time will tell which books are of lasting interest and importance, so keep this in mind when using price guides to set value to your stock.

The Books for Sale section of the trade papers is the most current source of price listings. You get to examine other dealers' prices without leaving your armchair.

Even after you've set a price for a particular book, it's not engraved in stone. You may change the price according to your market. For instance:

TRADE PAPERS: Books advertised in the larger and more prestigious publications can be set at full market value (retail) if the book is in demand and in exceptional condition, because thousands of potential customers screen these ads every week. More common books should be priced lower, since most of your potential customers are dealers.

BOOK FAIRS: The same applies, but be prepared to give a dealer discount.

FLEA MARKETS/GARAGE SALES: If you maintain a booth at a flea market or sell books periodically from your driveway, your prices will have to be set very low. Because you don't invest time and money in shipping, however, you can still make a profit with a minimal mark-up if you bought your stock at the right price.

QUOTING: If you happen to have specific titles which dealers have requested, either through want ads in the trades or want lists in the mail, you will prepare a "quote" detailing your book and setting your price. The dealer will, in turn, mark up this price to the customer to make a profit. Your price should be a "dealer" price, but not necessarily your lowest price since customers are special-ordering the book and should expect to pay full value to their dealer. A 20% discount off retail is reasonable for your quoted price, and the customer's dealer will pass it along for somewhat higher than retail. (More on quoting later.) If, however, the book you offer is a true

74

collector's item, scarce and in demand, you needn't lower the price at all. In a seller's market you can expect to get full retail, and the customer will pay a heftier premium and probably be glad to do so.

Customers seeking more common books, however, are not willing to fork over $20.00 for a book they envision gathering dust at the flea market for $5.00, no matter how much trouble and effort their dealer goes through. Human nature being what it is, all prices must be kept as low as possible or all parties involved are wasting their time.

While on the subject of quoting, there's a phrase you'll see in want ads that is rather controversial: "Priced for resale." That's a polite way dealers have of making the point that if your quoted price isn't low, don't bother to quote at all. Most often you'll see the phrase used when dealers look for books on a particular subject (ballet, chimpanzees, ice fishing, etc.) but don't specify titles. Any books you have on that subject can be quoted, keeping in mind that the dealer wants them for stock and expects to have room for a decent mark-up. (The term "priced for resale" is offensive to some quoting dealers as it vividly portrays the requesting dealer as a cheapskate unwilling to fork over fair value for books. They figure that since the books are obviously wanted for resale, quoting dealers should know enough to quote wholesale prices. The world, alas, is not realistic, and dealers are often deluged with books

priced through the roof. So they adopt
this catch-phrase as a warning.)

CATALOGS AND LISTS: When you put together a catalog or list of your books
in stock, your pricing will depend on
your intended customer. In the beginning you'll probably target other
dealers, as they're the most acces-
sible. If you offer common books, your
prices will have to be exceptionally
low (remember that urban bookshops can
be bombarded with people selling books,
and they needn't buy through the mails
at all). If you've been selective and
have good books in good shape, you can
ask more. Either build in a dealer's
discount, or make it clear at the top
of your list what your discount is.
Your competition is fierce, and the
more professional the appearance of
your mailing, the higher the prices can
be set. A fancy, offset and illustrated catalog can sell the same books for
more money than smudgy, mimeographed
sheets. "Image is everything" in the
buyer's mind, right or wrong.

Where to Price Your Books

Dealers usually use a soft-lead
pencil to write the price of each book
on the front free endpaper or the rear
endpaper. If the public rarely sees
your books, you may prefer to record
the price on an index card or slip of
paper and insert it between the front
endpapers. Other information can be
recorded on the card:

* important notes, such as "1st pr", or "sgd" if the book is autographed.

* your stock number, which comes in handy if you have several copies of the same title and want to tell them apart.

* a coded record of the price you paid. Take any arrangement of different ten letters, such as "ladyfinger", and assign the values of zero through nine (0-1-2-3, etc.). If you pay $3.50 for a book, write "YIL", or $10.00 would be "AL." The reason dealers use such codes is to save time. They can tell at a glance how much was paid for a book, which gives them a good idea what the lowest price can be to price a book, without having to search for receipts or trying to remember.

Once you sell a book by mail order, be sure to erase any markings you've made. Use a soft eraser (the pencil kind works well, especially white mylar erasers) and be careful not to ruffle the paper surface. It's better to leave writing in the book than to botch an erasing job. While we're on the subject, avoid the temptation to white out previous owners' names or to remove messy nameplates (unless a pro teaches you). You'll come across books where people have used scissors to remove the scars of previous ownership, but don't you ever do it. Another no-no is the use of price stickers. Even "removable" ones will adhere with time, and the damage they do to dust jackets is heart-breaking.

CHAPTER TWO

Where to Sell Your Books

Different dealers use different methods for selling. If you're a people person, all social and friendly-like, you might prefer having people come to your home. Depending on the restrictions of your community, you may want to advertise in the local paper and even post a sign at the end of your driveway. Once or twice a year you may want to hold a book sale in your garage or driveway. Such sales are a good way to clear your shelves of common books, paperbacks, book club editions, etc., that aren't worth the trouble of trying to sell by mail order. You might want to open a booth at the flea market during nice weather, or travel around to the various book fairs.

Less energetic people can rely on the mail and telephone. Ads can be placed in the trade papers for partic-ular titles for sale. You can produce a list or catalog of books and do a bulk mailing. You can quote your books individually to dealers seeking specific titles for their customers.

ADVERTISING IN THE TRADE PAPERS

Placing classifieds in the trade papers such as AB is the easiest way to sell used books if you've been careful to stock quality books that appeal to dealers and collectors alike. Trial and error can be costly, however, so be selective as to which books to offer

and how you describe them. Read the
current issues to see what's being
offered by others. Notice the format
and pricing.

Classified advertising is usually
charged by the line, and your books
will likely require two lines each to
properly describe. You might be able
to cleverly group books (such as first
American editions with dust jackets in
very good or better condition) and note
this in a heading before listing each
author and title on a single line.

Older or unusual books will need
several lines to describe, and with
advertising rates as high as a dollar
per line, you know you're only going to
offer books which merit the investment
and have generous mark-ups built in.

The types of books you offer through
classifieds will depend on which trade
paper you're using and current market
trends. AB appeals to many dealers and
collectors with money, and is a good
place to offer the cream of your literary crop. You'll see lots of limited
editions, autographed books and private
press titles offered in AB, and impressive price tags. Smaller circulation
papers, often with bargain rates, can
be used to sell less expensive books to
other dealers.

PLACING YOUR AD

Each trade paper will specify line
length -- the number of characters per
line of advertising (including spaces).
On a typewriter, space out the number
of characters and make a mark on your
paper, or set the margins on your word

processor to conform to the length.
Don't think you can squeeze in an extra
letter or two; you may find yourself
receiving an invoice from the paper if
you underpay.

Your first line will be your
business name, followed on the second
line by your address. For want ads you
may omit your telephone number, but
since most orders will be called in
(especially for your better books if
they're priced right), it's important
that a number be listed in your for
sale ads. On the third line, using
abbreviations (see the Appendix for a
list of standard abbreviations in the
trade), note your terms and conditions
of sale. You'll want people to prepay
for the books (CWO means "cash with
order"), and dealers calling you will
expect you to hold the book until their
checks arrive (specify how long you'll
wait for that check before you sell to
someone else). Prices listed in ads
are assumed to include postage. More
expensive books should also include the
cost of postal insurance. (Anyone
requiring UPS delivery should pay an
extra charge unless you routinely ship
by UPS.) Noting that the books you
sell are returnable will encourage
orders from people who have never heard
of you or are uncertain about the books
themselves, especially condition.
Every dealer has books returned at one
time or another. It's no big deal
(unless it's happening more than a few
times each year, in which case you'd
better determine why they're coming
back and then amend the situation).

Most dealers list their books with
the author's last name first (or at

times only the last name, especially if the author is famous), followed by the title. Then list the place of publication and the edition date (if you have a book printed in 1927, but the copyright is 1925, put 1927 in your ad). Don't bother to note the edition unless it's important. A book that does not have the edition noted is assumed <u>not</u> to be a first printing. If it is the first, say so. If you note only "1st", it's assumed to be the first American printing, in which case you may not need to list the year. Cheap books don't need as much information noted, such as the city or even the year.

Then note the condition of the book and any remarkable damage, and whether it's an ex-library copy, autographed, or whatever. If the dust jacket is present, note this, otherwise it's assumed there is no dust jacket. If the condition of the dust jacket is different than the book, note it, too. When describing the condition of your books, you may save money by lowering the total evaluation rather than describing every flaw (small spot on cover, front corner faded) and then adding "otherwise very good." Instead of "sm sp cvr, fr crnr fd o/w VG", simply judge the book as being in good condition, "G."

Certain assumptions are made that you should be aware of. Bindings are assumed to be hardback and original. Soft covers, rebindings and library bindings must be specified. Publishers are assumed to be original. Reprints, book club editions, foreign editions, etc., must be specified (the exception

being when a famous author has been
published by dozens of houses -- no one
will assume you're offering the first
printing of the original first edition
-- but you may need to specify the
publisher).

Dealers take many liberties for the
sake of economy. Your ad might appear
like this:

Joe Schmo, Bookman
POB 1, Anytown, Anystate 00000
(101) 555-5555, evenings
CWO, ppd, 10-day hold, returnable
Adams, Missy. To Catch a Butterfly.
  NY 1925 1st ed. dj. Fine $25
Bachelor, Michael. Mushrooms Can Be
  Fun. Boston 1949. 1st pr. color
  illustrations. spine warped. VG $80
Carboe. Get High from Life. Chicago 3rd
  pr 1965 dj autographed. Fine+ $10

Or this:

Joe Schmo, Bookman
POB 1, Anytown, Anystate 00000
(101) 555-5555, eve
CWO, ppd, 10-day hold, ret
Adams. To Catch Butterfly. 1st dj F $25
Bachelor. Mushrooms Can Be Fun. 1st clr
  ill, sp wrp. VG $80
Carboe. Get High fr/Life. dj sgd F+ $10

Don't go crazy cutting information
or you will find yourself cutting
sales. No one wants to telephone you
to learn what should have been specified in the first place.

Enclose full payment when you mail
in your ad. Once the trade paper gets
to know you and you prove to be reliable (i.e. keep your copy neat and

legible, preferably typed, and be sure
your check doesn't bounce), it might
set up an account for you so you're
billed monthly. This is a courtesy
that mustn't be abused.

You'll find that advertising rates
for nonsubscribers are usually so out-
of-proportion to the lower, subscriber
rates that if you plan on doing any
amount of advertising, fork over the
subscription ante.

When your ad breaks, try to stay at
home for the first couple days because
serious buyers will likely phone right
away and ask that you hold the books
until their checks arrive. Standard
holding time is one week to ten days,
and if you hear nothing by then, sell
the book with a free conscience to the
next caller. (Of course you'll take
down all callers' names and addresses,
if only to send them your catalogs).

If a buyer wants to return your
book, he should notify you in writing
or by telephone that the book is coming
back. Unsatisfactory condition is the
primary reason books are returned.
Sometimes the customer is too picky;
more often the dealer didn't evaluate
the book correctly or describe its
faults. Refund immediately, even if
not cheerfully. Then determine if you
were responsible for the book's
return. If a book comes back long
after the sale, or is damaged (and
you're not at fault, your original
packaging was secure), you have the
right to refuse a refund or remit a
lower amount.

Because of the high cost of
advertising in trade papers, this
method for selling books is not always

the best. It is, however, extremely
convenient when you consider the number
of hours it takes to put together a
catalog or lists, plus the added time
and expense to arrange addresses,
collate and stuff envelopes, apply
postage, etc. Analyze your own market,
try advertising once or twice, put out
one or two lists, and then make a
decision as to which tool will best
serve you.

CATALOGS AND LISTS

   You are in the mail order business,
right? Using the postal service as
your messenger, you must present your
product to a prospective customer,
establish its merit, weigh that against
its cost, and lure the person into
emptying his wallet into yours.
   You do this with a catalog or list
of the books you have for sale. They
are less work than quoting, cheaper
than advertising widely in the trade
papers (and they have a longer life-
span when it comes to future sales),
and give you more control over the
selection of targeted customers.
   Basically your business is no
different than those mail order houses
that fill your mailbox every day with
fancy four-color catalogs. They make a
visual statement that will catch the
recipient's attention and ('tis hoped)
hold it long enough to make an impact
so strong that it will be acted upon at
once. Because most bookdealer's catalogs are not illustrated, and their
lists almost never are, you have to

make your visual impact with a professional layout.

First, lists must be typed or
produced on a word processor. Yes,
you'll occasionally see hand-written
lists, but you won't be tempted to read
them. If you don't know how to type,
coerce your mate, beg your kid, or as a
last resort hire someone to type for
you. If all else fails, hunt-and-peck
or dig a "learn to type" book out of
stock and study it. One way or the
other, your lists must be typed.

Generous margins (when possible) and
accurate spelling lend to your credi-
bility. Don't crowd your listings.
Abbreviate when necessary, but don't
think that abbg ev wd wll mk u a pro.
Don't make your lists too difficult to
read.

Begin your list or catalog with a
section of "Terms & Conditions"
spelling out your business practices.
If you haven't included postage in the
price of your books (and I suggest you
do so since often people don't bother
adding it to the order), then outline
your scale of postage rates: $1.50 for
the first book, 50 cents each there-
after, for example. Specify your terms
for the return of books from unsatis-
fied customers. (Do you require prior
written notice? Will you give a full
refund, or deduct postage if you were
not at fault? Will you take returns
only within a specified time limit,
perhaps two weeks? Will you take a
book back for any reason, or only if
the buyer finds fault with your
description or some hidden flaw?)

Specify your policy for handling
telephone orders. How long will you

hold the book until a check arrives?
If you accept credit cards or fresh
postage stamps, or refuse both, put it
in writing. If you ship only by UPS,
you must let your buyers know so they
can include a street address with their
orders (UPS will not ship to a post
office box), or request that you use
the regular mails if they can't conveniently accept UPS delivery. If you
charge extra for insurance protection,
indicate the extra cost. Or you may
automatically insure orders with a
minimum value of, say, $30.00. What is
your policy for shipping to overseas
customers? Do you offer a dealer's
discount? (A rubber stamp reading
"Dealer Discount 20%" is helpful if
your mailing is divided between
collectors and members of the trade.)

You want to sweat these details at
the outset to avoid future misunder-
standings that aren't worth the time
and ulcers they can produce.

If your mailing is being sent only
to dealers, you can freely use abbreviations in your book descriptions without displaying an index as to their
meanings. You're discouraged from
inventing your own abbreviations. The
standard ones can be confusing enough,
as when a customer thinks "8vo" indicates an 8-volume set.

If your list is composed of a wide
variety of titles, separate them by
category: Westerns, Travel, Fiction,
Biography, etc. Traditionally books
are listed in alphabetical order by the
authors' last names. Book collectors
can easily scan for those authors they
collect. (On the other hand, dealers
are known to scramble their lists in

order to force customers to read through every title. This practice is not encouraged because it's apt to backfire when the busy customer tosses your list into the trash unread. Life's too short.) Truly fine items should be emphasized with a border or change in typeface.

Study the catalogs and lists you receive. Some will be as simple as mimeographed sheets, while others are fancy, typeset, annotated and illustrated. You'll be amazed at the inventiveness and wide range of layouts. Pick out a few that impress you and take them to your printer. He or she will be able to educate you on the economics of quick printing, if you're not experienced. Using standard paper sizes and formats, and light-weight paper when necessary, you can end up saving a great deal of money.

While laying out your own list or catalog, your first goal is clarity of communication, first in your book descriptions, and second in your presentation. Many customers appreciate larger type. You'll see catalogs where hundreds of listings have been reduced to fit a one ounce mailing, but you'd need a magnifying glass to read the descriptions. Lots of people won't bother.

You have many details to present about many books, and the method in which you type up this information can make a world of difference in how easily read it is. For instance, which one of the following has the clearest visual impact?

Carnegie, Wallace. Improve Your Life by
Eating Weeds. NY: Horticultural
Instit., 1908 (1906), 2nd ed. 8vo,
296pp, bds & cl, edges worn. Good+ $8

Carnegie, Wallace. IMPROVE YOUR LIFE
  BY EATING WEEDS. NY: Horticultural
  Instit., 1908 (1906), 2nd ed. 8vo,
  296pp, bds & cl, edges worn.
  Good+ $8.00

There are dozens of ways to empha-
size different pieces of information in
your listings using an ordinary typewriter. Look at how other dealers do
it, then copy the style of any that
impress you. No two dealers will type
up their information exactly alike.
(Special Supplement II details one
standard method for listing your
bibliographic information.)
Postage can cost you as much or more
than the actual printing of your lists,
so compact whenever possible without
cramming. Have your printer weigh your
mailing before running off all the
copies. If you can't get the list to
weigh less than one ounce or two
(depending on its bulk), either lower
the weight of the paper (from 20# to
16#, the lightest recommended if you're
printing both sides, as you should be)
or have the copy reduced. The few
dollars it costs for reduction should
be more than recovered in saved postage
costs. Be aware, too, that during
humid weather your catalog will weigh
more.
Envelopes cost a minimum of three
cents each. See if your format lends
itself to being a self-mailer. A list
consisting of four or five sheets can

be folded in half, stapled, and a blank panel used as the face for the address and postage. Lightweight papers are best used with an envelope, or at least tucked inside a heavier outside sheet. With regular typing paper and an envelope, you're restricted to four sheets to keep the weight below one ounce. Lose the envelope, and you can add an extra sheet.

One corner not to cut is postage. Always mail your catalogs and lists of books for sale by first class mail. Your customer in California isn't likely to waste a phone call to your New England number if it's obvious the east coast dealers have had your mailing a full week longer than the west coast dealers. Some booksellers won't even bother to read catalogs sent by third class bulk mail. (You are welcome to use bulk mail to send want lists and other advertisements.) If you're sending out numerous catalogs, contact your post office about their pre-sort first class mail rates.

Of primary importance is finding a reputable (and inexpensive) local printer. "Quick" printers now offer superior quality than in years past, and competition generally keeps prices low. Be sure to check with several printers and compare rates because the difference in prices can be staggering.

There are a number of other ways to produce your lists. You will not, of course, consider using a mimeograph process since legibility is necessary. Photocopiers are fast and reliable, and your second choice if a quick-print isn't convenient. You'll discover, however, that photocopiers are costly

machines if you're running off hundreds
of copies. Chemicals are incredibly
expensive, and "personal copiers" are
not built to take industrial abuse --
they overheat.

Keep track of your expenses and the
income produced by your catalogs. If
you're not making money, consider prac-
tical ways to economize. Are you carefully targeting your market? Are your
books priced high enough?

Your catalog or list is your calling
card to the trade. Be as professional
as possible. There is no excuse for
slipshod workmanship. Be assured that
with all the catalogs that deluge booksellers each week, time will not be
wasted in trying to decipher a sloppy
presentation.

Lists neatly put together and
offering books which are accurately and
completely described and reasonably
priced, are your best tool for making
multiple sales as a beginning bookseller.

THE ART OF QUOTING BOOKS

Before you organize your first list,
before you put together your first
classified ad for the trade papers --
get your feet wet by quoting. You can
start your whole book business with
exactly one book for one dealer who has
one paying customer who wants it. As
you are building stock and experience,
you'll be constantly quoting from want
ads in the trade papers and want lists
you receive in the mail.

As mentioned earlier, a brief
classified placed in AB or similar

publication will get you on the mailing
lists of several search services. Or
ask any established booksellers you
might know -- they're sure to receive
many each week.

Scan want lists as soon as they
arrive because the dealers are anxious
to receive quotes immediately, before
their customers have a chance to look
elsewhere for their books.

Only quote books which have a chance
to sell. You'll find that paperbacks
are marketable if priced low enough and
if they're in decent condition (but
don't price so low that you won't make
a profit).

Quote each book to only one dealer
at a time. This is professional
etiquette. You'll hear of great suc-
cesses where quoters have shotgun
multiple quotes for the same book, but
once booksellers and search services
catch on to who is doing this, these
shotgunners are likely to hit the "gray
list" and have doors closed on their
quotes. Too many disappointments follow when an order is returned because
you've sold the book to someone else
who was faster with the checkbook.

Whether or not you indicate on your
quote (and I suggest you do), set the
book aside for at least two weeks
before you offer it to someone else.
The dealer may have to contact an out-
of-state customer to get approval
before ordering.

Present your quote on a postcard or,
when quoting more than one title, index
cards. Postcards are a convenient size
and cost less to mail.

When quoting several books by the
same author, you can present them on

the same slip of paper. If the search service has numbered its want list, be sure to include this code. When responding to ads, name the publication and date as a reference. Above all, don't forget to include your own name and address!

What information do you include in your quote? Everything: Author's name, full title of the book, place of publication, publishing company, latest date and printing, edition if known, presence of a dust jacket, and an accurate appraisal of the book's condition. You will note, of course, whether the book is a paperback, book club edition, or ex-library copy.

Optional information is the book's size, number of pages, and a description of illustrations. As to noting the signatures of previous owners, use the same guidelines as when listing your book in a list, catalog or classified ad.

Quoted prices should always include postage. Expensive books should include the price of insurance or UPS shipping. Give the dealer one firm amount so there's no room for later misunderstanding. Here's an example of an acceptable quote:

QUOTING ... Want List #43, Item #12:

MacBeth, Harold. MEATBALLS AFLOAT. NY: Pearly Press, 1978 (1978, 1st pr). 8vo, 147pp + index. Illus w/b&w photos. Blue cloth w/gilt titles. Very good, bright condition in slightly worn dj.
Price ppd/returnable: $15.00 CWO
Will hold until July 25.

Joe Schmo, Bookman
P.O. Box 1
Anytown, Anystate   00000
(101) 555-5555

More and more quoters are using pre-printed forms for their quotes which spell out their terms and only need to have the blanks filled in with details of the particular item being quoted. These usually work well, although there has yet to be invented a standard format that will fit every title you have in stock. Computers are also pumping out quotes using standard formats, which is acceptable as long as they are readable.

Dealers love detailed quotes. If your wonderful and neatly typed or printed card offers a book for $10.00 in Good+ condition, and it's competing with a messy quote for the same book that states nothing more than the title and price -- you'll probably get the order even if the other promises a lower cost or a bit better condition.

Your quote leaves an impression of your professionalism, even if it proves unsuccessful (this time!).

BACKYARD BOOK SALES

If you live in a populated area, book sales in nice weather held in your driveway, garage or on your front porch can be profitable and fun. Your financial outlay will be in local advertising in the classifieds under "Garage Sales." If you'll be selling books of interest to homemakers (cookbooks, gardening, romance novels, etc.) or mass market paperbacks, mention them in your ad. You'll also plaster notices on every billboard in every grocery store and library for two counties around. If your books will not be set up under shelter, be sure to note a rain date in case of inclement weather. You can't risk water getting on your stock.

Only display the bottom of your book line because the sticky fingers of twelve-year-olds and the hot rays of the sun can do horrible things to your good books. If any serious collectors and dealers show up (and they will), get someone to cover the sale for you while you give them a private peek at your inventory, or pass out business cards and make appointments to show your better items at a later date.

Above all, keep your prices cheap! No one comes to a book sale to pay three dollars for a paperback. If you can't make a profit by selling paperbacks for a buck or less, or hardcover editions for around three dollars, then backyard sales are not for you.

Selling at flea markets is little different than in your backyard except you'll have to pay a table or booth fee to be included. Organize your books at least by subject, and make sure they are clean and their titles clearly displayed. Ragged books can be boxed together and priced at a quarter or fifty cents each, which always invites rummagers. If you can't bear to throw away books in truly poor shape, or which are realistically unsalable, set up a "free" table to draw people to your booth.

SCOUTING

Book scouts earn their daily bread by doing the bookdealer's footwork. There is no reason why you can't, too, as you're out stocking your own shelves.

First you must familiarize yourself with the subjects most handled by the dealers in your area. If one carries mostly fishing books, and another specializes in aviation, you'll keep your eyes open for books in these fields. If you discover a decent fishing book at what seems like a low price, you may want to buy it and trot it over to the respective dealer (with a stop at home to research its value). Keep in mind the price you'd like to receive for the book -- perhaps 50% of the estimated value -- or, if you don't know what it's worth, base the price on the minimum amount of profit desired.

Be prepared for disappointment. Numerous books on fishing are so common that dealers won't spend much, if anything, to stock them. Let the dealer make the first offer. He or she will probably explain the grounds on which the offer is based -- or why it is declined. Whether or not you choose to dicker depends much on personalities. If the dealer chooses not to buy the book, or the offer is simply too low, and you're not convinced that you could get a good price for the book by adding it to your regular stock, glance over the dealer's shelves and see if there's a nonfishing book you could swap. And don't leave before finding out what kinds of books the dealer desires. Most specialist booksellers maintain a "permanent want list" and would be happy to give you one.

CONSIGNMENTS

Sometime, someplace, someone is going to ask you to sell a book on consignment. If you don't have a policy against playing the middleman, here are a few basics.

First, make sure the book is salable and has some realistic value. If you can't gross a minimum of $50.00 (especially if you're working from your home and can't have the book on open display in a shop where it would sell itself), it's not worth your time and effort to handle.

Make sure the consigning party agrees that:

* You set the price, with no minimum.

* You have a certain amount of time in which to make a sale (one year is not too much).

* The "profit" is what remains after every penny of expenses is deducted from the gross. Besides advertising, don't forget little things like postage and phone calls, stationery, etc.

* Give yourself enough of a percentage to make your time worthwhile.

* If the book doesn't sell within the set amount of time, you will be paid for all expenses incurred. Be ready to itemize.

You can see why consignments are a
bother if you sell by mail order, and
are generally avoided.

BOOK FAIRS

Once you've gained some experience
selling books and learning the markets,
and once you've stocked at least 300
volumes priced at ten dollars and up,
you might consider participating in a
book fair. Most metropolitan areas
sponsor regional fairs open to any
exhibitor willing to pay the table
fee. You may have to be a member of a
bookdealer's association to participate
in larger shows, or pay a larger fee.
Fairs are so different in format and
rules that the best advice here is to
see to it that you know the rules and
do a little balancing of figures to
give you some idea of how much you'll
have to sell to make a profit. There's
no guarantee that the fair will be a
success, or that your booth will draw
as many customers as you'd hope.
You must consider the cost of
attending the fair. (Do you have to
take time off from your regular job?
Hire a baby-sitter? Travel far, with
the added expense of gasoline and
accommodations? Hire someone to help
with set-up?). Table fees can be
extremely high, meaning you'll need to
have many pricey books to sell. How
much of a loss could you handle, if the
sale falls flat? Find out how many
attendees are anticipated. If the fair
is an annual event, how many attended
in past years? Talk to dealers who
have exhibited before and see how eager

they are to exhibit again. Remember
that the success of the fair is not
dependent on how many books you sell,
but how many future contacts you culti-
vate. People you meet at the fair --
customers and dealers alike -- can be
valuable business assets in the future.

As an exhibitor, you will be provided with booth space and at least one
long table. You might be expected to
provide your own table coverings (which
are sometimes required to match those
of every dealer involved). Usually two
chairs are allotted per booth. If the
fair is for charity, you may be required to pitch in a percentage of your
gross sales. Food and drink are
usually available on the premises, but
check before you go. Give yourself
plenty of time to set up. You may be
competing with fellow dealers for dolly
carts and muscle to carry your stock to
your booth.

Book fairs are great fun, but not
every dealer finds them worthwhile.
The best way to test the waters is to
become involved with those which
present the least amount of financial
risk, then dig in with enthusiasm.

CHAPTER THREE

Mailing Lists and Packaging

A number of reference books are available that list nothing but names and addresses of fellow dealers, divided by their interests and location (see Appendix). Your investment in an up-to-date directory will be more than repaid with just one good mailing. Or you can pull names out of the trade papers to quickly develop a mailing list. How do you think your name is going to suddenly start attracting so much mail?

Make sure each mailing you send out reads "Address Correction Requested" beneath your return address so you'll be able to keep your list current. (Use it, too, for bulk mailings, but you'll be charged a small fee for each piece returned by the postal service.) Your mailing list is your lifeline to the outside world, so take particularly good care of it.

Remember that typed envelopes are processed more quickly through the mails, as they can be scanned by machinery. If you don't have use of a word processor, type the names on master sheets which can be photocopied onto labels. (See your stationery store or printer for more information.) For small mailing lists, alphabetical order may prove easiest to use. For bulk mailings, zip code order is preferred for ease in sorting. Mailing list services are available, and if money is no object and you get impatient with such business details, you may find it worth the money to recruit one.

Filling Orders

All the care you've taken with your
stock thus far should continue even
after the sale -- when you package up
the books. Invest in strong tape,
preferably the kind with filaments.
Post office personnel have not-so-nice
things to say about shiny tape, which
won't hold mailing labels or stamps
very well. Never use ordinary house-
hold transparent tape or masking tape
on the exterior of packages. Quality
tape is expensive but don't buy the
bargain tapes -- they're awful.

Examine each book before wrapping it
up. Remove your price if it happens to
be less than what your customer paid.
Remove smudges and fingerprints with a
soft eraser that leaves no colored
residue. Uncrease any folded pages.
Dust the edges.

Lay your receipt on top of the
cover, then wrap the book with a sheet
of clean paper. Almost any kind will
do, but never use newsprint. Ink
smears not only on your fingers, but on
the books themselves. Kraft paper,
wrapping paper, even paper towels if
that's all you have -- whatever is
handy so long as it's clean. Many
dealers use plastic bags or old manila
envelopes.

Follow this layer with a thick
padding of newspaper. (You may use
professional wrapping products such as
corrugated cardboard, "Jiffy Bags" and
bubble wrap, but they're costly.) Tape
the package securely, and write or
rubber stamp your address or your
customer's address on top. If you are
shipping a single volume that's not too

heavy, cover the thick padding with
strong brown paper, such as that used
for grocery bags. Neatly close up all
edges and ends with filament tape.
Corners should be smooth so they won't
catch and rip. The book should be
padded enough to resist punctures.

Heavy books should be wrapped as
above and packaged in a thick cardboard
box or, if too large, encased in layers
of cardboard. Newspaper balls or
recycled styrofoam "popcorn" should be
used to fill in all cavities so the
contents do not slide. When more than
one book is included in the box,
consider taping them together so they
don't rub against one another or get
separated should the box split. Don't
use dress boxes or cereal boxes as
mailing cartons. Paper towels do not
make good stuffing material. Avoid
using magazines or catalogs as padding
or liners -- they're heavy.

Avoid setting books on their spines
or edges unless they are thoroughly
padded. If you are sending many books,
break the order into boxes of 15 pounds
or less. (Overseas and Canadian orders
may be limited to 11 pounds to get the
best surface rates; check with your
local post office.) Of course you
could send one big box weighing 30
pounds and save a bit on shipping, but
a box that size is difficult to handle
and more likely to get dropped and
damaged. Wrap your books carefully
even when using padded mailers. If you
staple the end shut, cover the back of
the staples with tape to prevent
scratching.

Packages being mailed overseas (or
to the north during winter months)

should have a layer of plastic around the books. Many a soaked box has revealed a cozy and dry book due to the forethought of a wise bookseller.

You needn't invest in preprinted mailing labels, although they're inexpensive and give a professional polish to your shipments. Obviously you're going to carefully address packages, either writing directly on the outer wrapping with a black marker or using a label which is secured with clear tape.

Unless you're a fervid UPS customer, you'll be shipping by Fourth Class. Depending on the time of year and how far it's traveling, a book should take about a week to be delivered. You'll want to have a rubber stamp made up so you can mark each box with "Special 4th Class Book Rate" (don't leave out a single word; the P.O. can get finicky if it so chooses).

A single paperback may weigh so little that you'll send it by Priority Mail for the same cost, and on occasion Parcel Post is the better deal. A visit to your main post office will net you a booklet describing all the various rules and regulations, and showing current charges. While you're there, pick up a Zone Chart, so that if you ship Parcel Post to customers around the country, you'll be able to determine their zone and determine the cost. If you'll be shipping expensive books, pick up forms for insuring materials, or consider UPS.

When shipping more than one box to a customer, mark each box with a number, i.e. "#1 of 2." When shipping sets of books, get extra insurance coverage. The post office doesn't understand that

if a package breaks open and one volume
of a ten volume set is lost, the entire
set becomes worthless. They'll try to
reimburse you only 1/10th the insured
value.

You will want to establish a corner
of your home or office as a mail room.
You can purchase three-foot rolls of
brown paper for wrapping, and rolls of
tape purchased in bulk are very economi-
cal. You'll need an accurate mailing
scale (a ten pound scale is the most
helpful). Postage meters are inexpensive to rent and wonderfully convenient. (See "Pitney Bowes" in your
telephone white pages; don't let them
talk you into renting fancy equipment --
a bottom-of-the-line meter is more than
adequate.) The whole point to setting
up a mini-post office in your home is
to free you from having to truck down
to your neighborhood post office every
day and stand in line, arms ladened.
Your mail carrier can do the footwork,
or you can drop first class metered
mail right on the loading dock of your
post office night or day.

Fill orders promptly. Do not include correspondence unrelated to the
shipment (such as additional lists or
quotes) -- mail them separately in case
your package isn't immediately received
and opened.

Drop-Shipping

Frequently when you receive an order
in response to your quote, the dealer
will ask you to ship the book directly
to the customer. "Drop shipping" is a
standard procedure in the search ser-

vice business, but there is etiquette
to consider:

* Remove all your price indicators from
the book.

* Never include your own name and
address on the package, inside or out.
Use the dealer's address so if a return
is necessary, the book will go there.

* Accept any books returned by the
dealers and refund promptly. They are
shopping for their customers and your
quotes had better be accurate, but the
customer has the option of declining
the book for any reason whatsoever. In
all fairness, the dealer shouldn't
return the book to you if you were not
at fault (usually it can be absorbed
into stock). Fortunately, books are
rarely returned.

The purchasing dealer will likely
request that you confirm the shipping
date, and a stamped envelope or post
card should be included with the order
for this purpose.
Above all else, never, never, never
steal another dealer's customer. Sending your own catalogs to the drop-ship
address is a sure-fire way to get
yourself entrenched on the "gray list"
of suspect dealers.

CHAPTER FOUR

Running a Search Service

As soon as you hang out your shingle, people will be asking you to locate out-of-print books for them. The basic procedures are easy and can be very profitable. First, however, make sure your customer has a realistic idea of what an OP book will cost. If they expect to pay no more than four or five dollars (and many will, believe me), don't waste your time.

Many booksellers ask for a fee up front (usually a few bucks) before they search so even if a want ad fails to provide a quote, or if the customer changes his or her mind after the search has commenced, the bookseller at least breaks even. Other dealers gamble on success by offering a "free" search. The search isn't really free -- the fee is built into the price of the book after it is found and accepted by the customer.

If you seek only a few books for customers, you may do best to place the titles in a trade paper classified want ad -- the larger the circulation, the better. Don't get cheap when it comes to saving advertising money on your wants. You have to work quickly and efficiently to fill orders before your customers cool off. More common books will pull quotes in the smaller circulation papers. A weekly trade paper such as AB will present your wants more quickly than semi-monthly or monthly publications.

When listing titles in a trade paper, it's important to keep the information limited to one line. Frequently you can omit the author's first name, or shorten the title. If your customer wants a hardcover copy of any edition of the book, this is all the information you need to list. If, however, he specifically requests a first edition, a paperback, or a dust jacket, then note this in your listing. If you know he wants the cheapest copy obtainable regardless of condition, then put "rc" (reading copy) in the ad so dealers with fine first editions won't waste their time quoting to you.

Quotes should start arriving soon after your ad breaks. Set them aside for a week (unless the perfect quote comes right away -- no point in waiting and risking the book's prior sale to someone else; remember, not all quoters hold their books for the standard two weeks). Then call or write to your customer and offer the best copy (or give him a choice if there are enough differences between the quotes), and firmly request an immediate decision -- and payment.

The price to your customer should include:

* the cost of the book from the quoting dealer,

* a profitable mark-up (your fee),

* all expenses, particularly advertising, and

* local taxes if applicable.

Quote your customers one lump price,
noting that it's "complete" so they
don't think your fee or postage is
extra.

If you buy a book from a quote for
$5.00 and your expenses total $1.75,
you should price the book at no less
than $12.00 ($15.00 would be better,
and lower the price to $10.00 only if
your customer won't consider anything
over that -- people sometimes get very
tight with money despite their urgency
when placing the order).

If you happen to know that the book
you bought for $5.00 is genuinely more
valuable -- let's say your research
shows that it should have been priced
at $25.00 -- then by all means up the
price to fair market value. Such
financial shots in the arm help offset
the all-too-common losses.

Booksellers operate search services
very differently. For instance, some
order from the first good quote without
obtaining permission from the customer,
thereby eliminating the risk of prior
sale but gambling that the customer
will accept the book. This practice is
not recommended unless you know your
customer well or are prepared to absorb
the book into stock should it be declined. (You have no grounds to return it
to the quoting dealer if he has no
fault in the matter.)

If you receive only one quote for a
book but it's priced so high your customer balks, it doesn't hurt to write
to the quoting dealer and suggest a
reasonable counter-offer. Don't get in
the habit of doing this, but occasionally it will seal a deal that might
otherwise have fallen through.

With the cost of advertising so high
and increasing each year, be sure your
customer is serious, and don't advertise repeatedly if you don't have the
money up front to cover your costs.
You might even be able to track down a
book without going through the slow
process of advertising by dropping an
inquiry to a dealer specializing in the
subject of the book. Check your
directory of booksellers under subject
heading, and be sure to include a self-
addressed stamped envelope if you
expect a reply. In fact, always
include SASE if you want a reply to any
kind of important correspondence.

If you have numerous books to
locate, consider putting together a
want list and circulating it to every
bookseller and scout you communicate
with. Add one to every piece of
correspondence you send out. If you
are seeking more than fifty titles,
consider a mass mailing to dealers who
have quoted to you in the past. A bulk
mailing to 200 dealers is very inexpensive -- much cheaper than running a
trade paper ad, and your mailing will
get more direct attention than an ad.
Be sure to scratch out those titles no
longer needed so dealers won't waste
their time and postage responding
unnecessarily.

If you can't find a customer's book
within a year, find out if you should
continue searching. You may want to
ask for enough money to cover all past
expenses and future advertising, since
a book which hasn't surfaced in so long
is unlikely to suddenly surface, although it happens. When the book
finally shows up, expect the price to

be steeper than for a common book. A
good suggestion is to "clean house"
once a year (January is an ideal time)
by contacting every search service
customer to see if he or she still
requires your services. It's also
frustrating to locate a book, and then
find you can't locate your customer.

When ordering books for your customers, be sure to enclose payment in
advance. Instruct the dealer to drop-
ship the book directly to your customer
unless the book can conveniently be
picked up at your home. Enclose an
SASE or SASPC (self-addressed stamped
postcard) for confirmation of shipment
date. Your SASE will also be necessary
in the event the book has already been
sold and your check is returned.

Some search services dispense with
stock and concentrate on filling
orders. Other booksellers find that
the details necessary for running a
search service are so mind-boggling
that after awhile they drop out. If
you can't make a profit running a
search service as part of your bookselling efforts, narrow your sights to
other methods of making money with used
books.

Section IV

PAPERWORK!

The foundation upon which your business rests is paperwork. Your image is projected mostly through the mails, so your choice of stationery, business cards, etc., is important. An accurate record-keeping system is paramount to your success. Although we envy the dealer who at a snap remembers every customer, every want, every book in and out of stock (and whose habit of using old hotel stationery is excused as a humorous eccentricity) -- most of us need to be more conventional.

A Name for Your Business

Before you can worry about ordering rubber stamps and business cards, you need to decide on a business name. As you examine the trade papers, you'll notice an amazing variety of bookseller names. Some are cute, others clever, some sophisticated, and many simple and straight forward. The most common form of name for the home-based bookseller is the owner's own name. Such a moniker is unpretentious and clear:

Joe Schmo, Fine Books

J. Schmo, Bookseller

Joseph Schmo First Editions

Schmo Used Books

Find a business name that is suitable and comfortable. Don't let it overstate your knowledge (J. Schmo Rare Books) or be too difficult to spell (O-Kee-Fen-O-Kee Bookerama). You hope your name will be memorable. Try to avoid names that play off the letter B -- "Bargain Books", "Book Basement", etc. You'll have a hard time coming up with something that hasn't been done repeatedly, and the name will likely be less memorable since it's too similar to others.

In some states you'll have to register your name on a county level before being able to open a business checking account, and at the state level to collect required sales tax. Check the government listings in your telephone book. The forms are quick and easy to fill out.

You will have to apply to your state's department of finance to be assigned a "resale number" required by any merchant who buys inventory within the state. In turn, all your customers will pay retail tax to you unless:

* they are dealers who can produce a resale number.

* shipment is made out-of-state or out of the country.

* they are a library, university, or other nonprofit organization.

Keep track of the amount of taxes collected and filling out forms for your state's retail tax office will be a simple procedure. If possible, try to get on a yearly payment schedule so you don't have to bother with monthly or quarterly forms. Chances are that as a beginning bookseller, you'll not collect the minimum amount requiring more frequent filing.

Logos

The bookselling world is sadly deplete in catchy logos, which is exactly why they can be so important. You want your business to be remembered. If your company name lacks the punch to permanently adhere to the little gray cells of every dealer and collector who sees it, then design a logo that will. For a minor, one-time "set-up" charge, the trade papers will put your logo on any full-page or display ad you submit, and because so few dealers use them, your logo will draw immediate attention to your ads.

A logo can embellish your stationery and checks. Design or select a simple one, a clear line-drawing, black-on-white. A poorly executed logo will be remembered for the wrong reasons. If you don't have the skill to do the job right, get a graphic artist to do it for you. Take the finished drawing to your local printer and have it reduced to various sizes ranging from half an inch to a couple inches, then have several camera-ready copies made. That way you'll always have one on hand when needed. You can also have your logo put on a rubber stamp for customizing mailings.

Opening a Checking Account

Because your business will be conducted through the mails, you'll be dealing with more checks than cash. One advantage to using your own name as the company title is that you might be able to maintain a personal checking account at your local bank and save a lot of money in checking charges. Shop around because there's a wide range of fees between banks.

Your bank is likely to charge up to several cents for each deposit total you add to your account, and perhaps a few cents for each individual check which makes up the total. Because you'll be dealing with numerous small checks, both coming in and going out, you may save a great deal by finding a bank that charges a set monthly fee.

Stationery and Business Cards

Economy is very important as you begin your bookselling adventure, and stationery is one place where you can effectively cut corners. If you choose not to have expensive imprinted stationery, remember:

* Rubber stamps (black or blue ink, and with a very legible block typeface) can turn plain paper and envelopes into very acceptable stationery.

* If you have attractive and easy-to-read handwriting, and lots of extra time, you may choose to forego stationery altogether. You'll have to be particularly careful not to omit your

name and address from quotes and
correspondence. Typewritten communica-
tions are much preferred, however.

* Forms such as invoices, purchase
orders, postcards and memos can be
purchased blank and personalized with
your rubber stamp. Or find the forms
most appropriate to your business in
one of the popular books of generic
forms. Type in your name and address
and have your printer run off copies on
white or colored paper. The cost is
minimal.

However optional imprinted stationery might be, professional business
cards are a must. If you have a logo,
use it. Choose a bold, simple style
that emphasizes professionalism over
cuteness. Check with at least three
printers (and ask specifically if they
do their own printing or if they send
it out, as is commonly done even by
commercial printers). Ask to examine
paper samples and colors. Don't
automatically select the cheapest price
until you've weighed the variables.
Once you've settled on a printer,
lay out your copy as much like the
finished product as possible. Type
your copy and proofread it over and
over again. Printers will hang onto
instructions for as long as a year just
in case they have to prove that any
errors in the final copy were your
fault. Keep a photocopy of your
instructions in your files.
Don't be talked into ordering more
cards than you'll need over the next
year or two. As a beginner, you can't
anticipate changes you'll make later

such as a new name, the addition of
services to your business, or a move
into a bookshop -- all of which could
entail new cards.

Besides the usual facts, you might
consider including on your business
cards the types of books you want most
to buy and sell, mention of a search
service or appraisal service (once you
have enough experience), and perhaps a
small map or instructions if you're
open to the public and difficult to
find.

Personal vs Business Telephones

Because there are so many home-based
booksellers in this country, you do not
require a separate phone for your
business in order to be professional.
Collectors and dealers calling to place
orders are not surprised when children
answer or a television is bellowing in
the background. Save the money and use
your personal telephone unless you plan
to do a lot of local business. A business telephone automatically entitles
you to a listing in the Yellow Pages,
which is terrific advertising if your
business slants that way. Be fore-
warned that the phone company doesn't
want you to run a business on your
personal line, and they catch mis-
creants by checking the phone numbers
in newspaper classified advertisements
obviously placed by small businesses.

Office Equipment

Your primary piece of office equipment is a typewriter. Typed envelopes are processed more quickly by the postal service. Typed quotes are more welcomed by dealers. Even pretty and artistic handwriting can be difficult to read.

A telephone answering machine is very convenient if you aren't at home during the day. If you have a Books For Sale ad running, or a list being circulated, you might even be able to quickly specify in your message which books are no longer available so the caller won't leave a message if he's missed out. Since most of your buyers will try to call, you're risking a lot of lost profits by not being able to take the calls one way or the other.

If a potential customer leaves a long-distance telephone number, you may balk at paying the toll charges to return the call. If you are calling to confirm a sale and request a check, you pay for the call. (Obviously you're not expected to pay for calls overseas unless the book involved is a valuable one.) You do not have to call back at all if the book requested is already sold. The customer will know that your lack of response means the item has been previously grabbed. Whether you pay for returning cold calls, where you have no idea why the person telephoned, use your discretion.

Whenever possible, find out what other books might be of interest to the caller. One sale may have fallen through, but the contact could be important for the future.

The most convenient piece of office
equipment you could own is a photo-
copier. Prices have dropped consider-
ably in recent years, and the machines
are smaller and faster. Short-run
mailings such as want lists can be
efficiently and quickly produced with a
quality copier. When pricing copiers,
compare the following:

* simplicity of use,

* speed and quality of copies,

* paper size and quality specifica-
tions,

* recommended maximum number of copies
(monthly),

* basic cost of the machine,

* length and coverage of warranty,

* cost of developer, toner, dry imager,
etc., and the number of copies they'll
produce (keeping in mind that this number is based on the size of an average
business letter, which doesn't cover
much of a page; you may realistically
cut in half the number of copies
promised by your sales rep),

* availability and cost of local repair
service,

* simplicity of use, and

* availability and cost of a service
contract.

You will, of course, consider only a "dry" process so you can print on a variety of papers, including colored stock and stationery. Avoid machines requiring coated papers or rolled paper. It's unlikely you'll need reducing/enlarging capabilities, or other advanced features which inflate the price.

You'll find that inexpensive machines -- under $2,000 -- may not take heavy use, as they will overheat and shut down. If you're mechanically inclined, you may wish to forego an extended service contract (which can cost a few hundred dollars yearly). You'll find that service calls can cost you from $50-$200+ just to get a repair person to show up, so weigh your decision carefully. (Using developer, etc., not sold by the manufacturer, or calling a generic copier repair service, can damage the machine and/or invalidate any warranty.) Used copiers are not a good idea, but you might be able to purchase a rebuilt machine that carries a full warranty. When buying any piece of office equipment, you'd be wise to consult Consumer Reports (at your library).

You may have fond childhood memories of aromatic mimeographic sheets with the fuzzy blue ink, but they are not acceptable in the bookselling world. Yes, a few dealers use them. And lots of other dealers won't strain their eyes trying to read them.

The hottest piece of equipment in the bookselling business is, of course, the computer. A separate chapter addresses the many intricacies of

selecting hardware and software for
your new company.

Fax machines are being used by some
dealers now, and likely we'll see them
used even more in the years ahead.
Imagine the advantage of faxing book
quotes, where time may be of the
essence.

Other types of small equipment
you'll need are obvious: a pencil
sharpener, stapler, furniture, calcu-
lator, file cabinets, etc. Don't go
hog wild in the beginning. Put your
money into more important things like
reference books, quality stock, and
effective advertising. One advantage
to working out of your home, away from
the public eye, is that you can work on
a make-shift basis while you grow. You
don't have to pay for professional
cosmetic dressing, as long as your
procedures are professional.

Don't neglect the tax write-off
you'll get from money invested in equipment. Keep all your receipts! And
because you'll be working from a
dedicated space in your home, you
should be able to deduct a percentage
for your office and library.

Inventory and Other Records

As each book comes into stock,
you'll need a written record of all its
features, what you paid for it, what
your asking price is, and all data your
research turns up. You may also want
to indicate the category you've chosen
for the book. Don't discount this
important fact since books have a habit
of straddling subjects, and you'll want

to know where you've shelved it. If
you assign stock numbers to the
individual books, include them in the
record. If you're using a manual
system, an index card is a good size
for recording this information. If you
use a bibliographic format, the text
can be duplicated word-for-word in your
catalog.

When a book sells, pull the card and
record the date of the sale, the name
and address of the buyer, and the
price. File the card for future reference (in case you can quote something
similar to the same customer, or in
case the same title should come into
stock again and you'll not have to
duplicate research).

Keep a close record of those books
quoted out to dealers which are on
hold. Either record your quote somewhere on the card (with the dealer's
name, date quoted, and quoted price),
or keep a separate list. You probably
won't have to physically pull the book
from the shelf if your stock is not
open to the public.

You will want a system for keeping
track of your customers. This is
easily done with a computer and database software. In either case, you
will want to have a way of accessing
lists of dealers who quote to you,
customers who are collectors, and those
people who share your major interest or
specialty. Set up a system before you
launch your business, otherwise you'll
soon find yourself up to your successful neck in paperwork and it will be
difficult and discouraging to dig out
of it at a later date. Oil your wheels
first! And if your original system

doesn't work, alter it until it does.
Keep it simple or you'll be more apt to
neglect the upkeep as time passes.

The most important file on your desk
is the one marked "Pending." This will
include purchase orders awaiting delivery, copies of auction bids awaiting
response, copies of your correspondence
awaiting replies, search service offers
awaiting approval, perhaps a list of
books quoted out -- anything that needs
further input before you can terminate
the transaction. Check this file every
single day.

You will also need a filing system
that makes any piece of paper quickly
retrievable should it prove necessary.

Of course some dealers, particularly
old-timers, don't bother with paperwork
at all. This "hobby" attitude won't
suit a growing business in this day and
age of spreadsheets and business plans.
You don't have to go that far to run a
successful bookselling operation, but
good business practices will give your
company a solid foundation.

Very important: Keep your paperwork
up-to-date. Answer your correspondence
promptly, and pay your bills right
away. Keep your commitments to
customers and fellow dealers. Remember
always that you are running a business,
and even if it's not a multi-million
dollar corporation, treat it with just
as much respect. That means you must
realize your own importance and carry
on with self respect and faith in your
abilities.

THE FUTURE OF BOOKSELLING

You are entering a field that is
growing daily, but not as much as the
demand it serves. Our government has
put the squeeze on publishers, meaning
they must clear out their warehouses on
newly printed books to avoid paying
high taxes on inventory. The number of
books printed has been cut in order to
reduce these inventories, and books are
going out of print faster.

Recently a clerk at a new bookstore
told a customer, "Are you kidding?
That book was published over six months
ago -- of course it's out of print."

Understand? You've got a big job to
do!

More and more new bookstores are
getting into the OP market by offering
a search service to their customers.
Rather than viewing them as competition, see if you can't help supply
their wants. Be flexible, willing, and
hard-working -- you can't help but do
well and make money.

Modern technology is hammering away
at the dusty, dark bookshop image of
days gone by. Computer software has
been designed especially for booksellers. More and more dealers are computerizing their inventory, even the
smallest of businesses. Mailing list
maintenance is simple, accurate and
fast. Quotes are quick and easy to
produce. Word processors make your
catalogs a snap to produce camera-
ready, and as books are sold and
removed from stock, your lists are
automatically renumbered and inventory
records brought up-to-date.

Don't be put off by this technology
if you're planning to work from your
kitchen table using file boxes and
index cards. Thousands of folks in the
business are perfectly happy hand-print-
ing quotes and typing up lists of books
for sale on an old, manual Underwood.
The beauty of this business is that
even the most backward of procedures
can bring success as long as the
business is handled professionally --
which is more an attitude than anything
else. The results will be same: You
will enjoy immense satisfaction putting
books into the hands of excited and
appreciative customers. You will know
the joy of locating books that couldn't
be found, and unearthing treasures in
the oddest of places. As a vital
middleman or middlewoman, your job is
important, rewarding, and profitable.
Now get going -- make a buck, sell a
book!

Special Supplements

Appendix

This Special Supplement is intended as an introduction to computers and their application to the book world for those of you agonizing over whether to buy or not to buy, along with suggestions in case you've already taken the plunge.

If you're serious about purchasing a system for your business, it's vital that you educate yourself -- and we admit that's no easy task with so many choices out there. Arm yourself with a thorough understanding of what you need a computer to do for you and your business, and don't let yourself be distracted from your purpose.

Read the many magazines on the subject and study their recommendations. Talk to people who know computers and software, and don't be afraid to ask what might seem like stupid questions. Insist on demonstrations, and don't get swept away by flashy jargon and expensive ad campaigns.

Frustration and anger will dominate your relationship with your computer during the first year. This is normal. Hang in there and we promise you'll be rewarded in the long run with increased efficiency, expanded abilities, and (yes!) _fun_.

COMPUTERS IN THE BOOK WORLD

Steven W. Bare and D. Keith Crotz

The Basics

WHAT MAKES A COMPUTER COMPUTE?

A PERSONAL COMPUTER is a computer built around a single microprocessor. The microprocessor is the "brain" of the computer and performs all of the logical operations and calculations. It is part of the central processing unit (CPU). Other PC components include memory, the keyboard, disk drives and a monitor.

The driving force of increased performance in microcomputers has been the development of faster and more powerful microprocessors. The first IBM PCs and compatibles were built around the Intel 8088 processor. The IBM-AT and compatibles were designed around the Intel 80286 processor. The Intel 80386 processor was developed and appeared first in Compaq computers and later in some of the IBM-PS/2 computers. The Intel 80486 processor has been developed and will bring the power of mainframe computers to the desktop. Each new processor has provided far greater processing capacity. However, it is not the sole determinant of system performance.

Internal memory is the part of the computer where data is temporarily stored. It may be thought of as a desktop where you place items that you need to work with. The disk drives could be thought of as filing cabinets where information is stored when it is not on your desktop. When you need to process an item, the program moves it from the disk (the filing cabinet) to memory (the desktop).

Internal memory is divided into two areas: "read only memory" (ROM), and "random access memory" (RAM). ROM is used by the operating system, the programs that control the computer. RAM is used as a temporary storage location for data. Standard systems today contain 6740 K or 1024 K (1 megabyte) of memory.

The smallest denomination in the world of computers is the "bit." The bit is a binary character, either a zero or a one. By combining eight bits we can represent one alphanumeric character (a letter or number) which we in turn call a "byte." One thousand bytes is represented by 1 K or 1 K bytes. One meg or 1 megabyte represents one million bytes. So, when we talk about memory, 640 K is 640,000 bytes, and 1 megabyte is 1,024,000 bytes (rounded to 1,000,000 for convenience). The length of this chapter is approximately 12 K.

There are a number of factors which affect the performance of the personal computer. First and foremost is the processor. Processor performance is determined by its speed and the width of its data path. Processor speeds are measured in megahertz -- millions of cycles per second. The width of the data path is measured by the amount of data it will accept at a time. An 8-bit processor will accept one byte of data at a time, a 16-bit will accept

two bytes, and a 32-bit will accept
four. You might think of it as the
difference between the volume of traf-
fic that can travel a one-, two- or
four-lane highway. Following is a list
of processors, their speed in megahertz, and width of each data path:

Processor / Megahertz / Width data path

8088	4.77, 6 or 8	8-bit
80286	8, 10 or 12	16-bit
80386	6, 20, 25 or 33	32-bit

You can see how combinations of
processor speed and width of data path
create a tremendous difference in
performance of the various processors.

Disk Drives

DISK DRIVES are available in two
major types: floppy disks and hard
disks. Floppy disks are either 3-1/2
inches or 5-1/4 inches in diameter.
They are removable from the drive and
are used for storing small amounts of
data. The 3-1/2 inch disks are
available in either 720 K or 1.4
megabyte formats. The 5-1/4 inch disks
are available in either 360 K or 1.2
megabyte formats. The 3-1/2 inch
floppies are fast becoming the standard
format.
Hard disks are internal,
nonremovable disk drives. The storage
capacities vary from 10 megabytes to
more than 100 megabytes. Generally, a
30- to 40-megabyte hard disk will
provide all the storage you need unless
you process very high volumes of data.

Disk performance is measured by the
speed with which you can access data on
the disk. Common access speeds today
run from 100 milliseconds (100
thousandths of a second, slow) to 20
milliseconds (fast). Slow and fast are
relative to the current state of the
industry. Several years ago 100
millisecond drives seemed blindingly
fast.

Keyboards

KEYBOARDS are relatively standard
and have not enjoyed as much progress
as other PC components. Typical config-
urations today are 84-key and 101-key
keyboards, each with 12 function keys.
I prefer the 101-key model with its
separate keys for controlling cursor
movement.

Monitors

MONITORS, the TV-type display which
you read, are really a combination of
two components: the monitor and the
video adapter. Monitors either display
one color (monochrome) or many colors
(color monitors). The type of video
adapter determines whether or not you
can display color on a color monitor.
The standard video adapters today are
the monochrome display adapter (MDA),
color graphics adapter (CGA), enhanced
graphics adapter (EGA), and video
graphics array (VGA). As you move
through the list, the adapters become
more sophisticated, provide higher
resolution and display more colors.

In most business applications it is difficult to justify the cost of the high-end color monitors and adapters. Usually the best price performance ratio for general business use is achieved by combining a monochrome display adapter with a good quality monochrome monitor.

Printers

The printers most commonly sold today are dot matrix, daisy wheel and laser printers.

DOT MATRIX PRINTERS form each character by printing a matrix of dots. The print heads for these printers contain either 9 or 25 pins which press against a ribbon in various combinations to form individual letters. These are great all-around printers and are available from two hundred dollars to a thousand dollars or so. They do not provide true letter-quality print.

DAISY WHEEL PRINTERS are little more than typewriters that can be hooked up to your word processor. Although they are truly "letter quality", they are slow and require a good deal of maintenance. Because they are inexpensive, however, they make a viable addition to your dot matrix printer for times when appearance is important, as when producing catalog copy or material to be reproduced at your local printshop.

LASER PRINTERS are true letter-quality printers. Rather than print

characters one at a time, they create
the image of an entire page and then
print the full page. The workings of a
laser printer are very similar to a
photocopy machine. With the prices of
these printers down to one to two
thousand dollars, they are a realistic
option when true letter quality is
important. They first gained popularity in desktop publishing systems.
Some softwares, however, are not
adaptable to laser printers, although
they are quickly catching up to this
popular newcomer.

PURCHASING YOUR FIRST COMPUTER

We firmly believe in buying name
brand computers from local dealers.
Usually service, support and trouble-
free operation are worth the extra
price attached to a name. IBM, Compaq,
Epson -- all are available from local
dealers and distributors. The mail
order bargains you'll find in the back
of magazines can often save money up
front -- but who will help you format
the hard drive and load the config.sys
file when the machine arrives? If you
don't have the experience, play it safe
the first time.
Buying your computer from a local
authorized dealer ought to provide you
with competent support for the future.
Being able to take classes for word
processing and in DOS from the store
where the equipment was purchased is a
bonus for the computer illiterate.
Computer classes are a must for those
who want to make computerization a
little less painful. If nothing else,

the classes should provide you with a
manual put together by the instructor
which will make finding commands and
methods much easier than agonizing
through the DOS manual that arrives
with your machine.

Don't crowd yourself. Provide a
dedicated work area for the new
devices. You'll be more inclined to
use your new technological wonder if
you have easy and immediate access.

Turn it on each day. You'll
initially sit and stare at the blank
screen. It's at this point that you
realize this new contraption can't do a
single thing for your book business
until you've put some book-related data
into its memory.

Software

For letters, stories or notes to
yourself, I recommend WordPerfect.
I've tried WordStar, MultiMate, and for
whatever personal prejudice, settled on
the former because of its many special
features. [Editor - WordPerfect is
fast becoming the industry standard for
word processing.]

One of these features is the ability
to use WordPerfect as a database for
sorting bibliographic data and wants.
This feature is available out of the
box and requires no special reprogram-
ming on your part. Called Mail Merge,
this unique function allows reports,
lists, and even inventory items to be
sorted, listed, combined, even printed
in about any order you like in any form
you choose. All you have to do is
enter the data in a consistent manner.

The on-line help screen function is very useful and easy to follow. I rarely have to consult the cumbersome manual.

Special Bookseller Software

In order to track your inventory, generate catalogs, mailing lists and quotes, special dedicated programs are recommended. They are available in a wide range of prices and ease of use.

Notebook is the least expensive at $175. It arrives with fairly simple instructions, ease of data entry and fast access to your inventory. Many of these files you must design yourself though, and I've had trouble getting the data to print out in the style and order requested. Notebook, to my knowledge, does not generate invoices, wants, or other customer information. Such applications must be acquired elsewhere.

The high end of the spectrum comes from Book-ease. I've played with this ultra-expensive (around $3,000) inte-grated software program that will generate catalogs, track quotes and wants, create invoices, mailing lists and just about anything else associated with bookselling. My personal feeling is that the program is not the least bit user friendly, and the manual is difficult to follow.

After a long search, I settled on BookBase. It produces a catalog of 400 titles by subject criteria in less than 30 minutes. Your only role, as a book-seller, is to faithfully enter each title into inventory. Don't get behind

-- catch-up is an evil game to play.
The drawback of this program is an
alphabetized mailing list based on the
first name only, which takes time to
get used to. This software, at $675,
will track sales, inventory, quotes,
wants, and even display outstanding
invoices and sales by categories. All
in all, the program will streamline
your business.

COMPUTERIZING YOUR BUSINESS

Getting your inventory computerized
will require huge amounts of time and
discipline. It will take effort and is
not the great immediate panacea that
many tell you it can be. The rewards
will take several months to see.
I cannot stress enough the importance of backing up your system on a
regular basis. This process involves
making archival copies of the data and
programs on your hard disk. The backup
utility creates a copy of the hard disk
on a series of floppy disks. When (not
if!) your hard disk fails, you will
have all your data and programs available to quickly and accurately restore
the hard disk.
The operating system (DOS -- Disk
Operating System) that comes with your
computer includes a backup command to
transfer data from the hard disk to
floppies. I prefer the backup program
included with PC Tools Deluxe, published by Central Point Software and
available at your local computer
center. It performs the backup at a
much higher speed and has a verify
option to test the integrity of your

backup. I had several instances where
the DOS backup failed and I was not
aware of it until I needed to restore
data. This problem has not occurred
since I switched to PC Tools and used
the verify option.

   To summarize, using PCs to automate
tasks in your enterprise can offer
significant increases in productivity.
The real payback, however, is in having
the ability to track and analyze data
that you could not before. Use your PC
as a means of learning more about your
customers' buying habits and wants.
Target mailings to customers who buy
specific types of books. The uses are
limited only by your imagination.

* * * * *

Contact the following companies for
further information and prices for
bookselling software:

[Apple]
TaBiblio
Turnkey Technologies
P.O. Box 1071
Larchmont, New York   10538

[IBM & Compatibles]

BookBase
H. & J. Price Company
1520 Crest Road
Silver Springs, Maryland   20902

NoteBook II
Pro/Tem Software, Inc.
814 Tolman Drive
Stanford, California   94305

Book-ease
Columbia Computer Consultants
670 Waters Edge
Valley Cottage, New York   10989

* * * * *

WRITING A BIBLIOGRAPHIC DESCRIPTION

A complete bibliographic description of a book will include, in this order:

1) Author (last name first)
2) Book title + subtitle
3) Number of volumes (sets are assumed complete unless you say they're not)
4) Place of publication
5) Publishing company
6) Date on title page (if present)
7) Latest date, edition and/or printing on copyright page (place it in parentheses)
8) Known edition, state, issue or printing, but not stated outright in the book [place it in brackets]
9) Copy number and number of copies printed, if a limited edition
10) Size of book
11) Number of text pages + advertising pages (if present)
12) Type of illustrations + illustrator (if known and relevant)
13) Binding color and type (optional unless necessary to distinguish a point or add to the book's salability, as with leather covers or special artwork)
14) Description of edges (inked, if relevant, or gilt; untrimmed, unopened or deckled)
15) Notes of importance concerning the physical text of the book (marbled endpapers, hand-colored title page, folding map laid in, etc.)
16) Description of condition, notation of flaws

17) Presence and condition of dust jacket, slipcase or box
18) Overall evaluation of condition
19) Presence of author's signature or similar association interest
20) Bibliographic reference, if relevant [place in brackets]
21) Any interesting information you may wish to share about the book or its author
22) Price

Rarely will you need to list all the above items when describing one book, except perhaps for your own information on your inventory card.

Here's an example of basic bibliographic information about one book, and the different forms used for different applications:

Full information:

Barrie, J.M. SENTIMENTAL TOMMY. The Story of his Boyhood. Published in New York by Charles Scribner's Sons, 1896 (1896) [1st edition]. 12mo, 478pp. Black & white plates by William Hatherell. Brown decorated cloth. Ink presentation by previous owner. Very good condition. Listed in Cutler bibliography of J.M. Barrie. $--.--

Catalog description:

Barrie, J.M. SENTIMENTAL TOMMY. The Story of his Boyhood. NY: Scrib-

ner's, 1896 (1896) [1st ed]. 12mo,
478pp. b&w plts by Wm Hatherell.
brown deco cl. ink pres. VG
[Cutler] .... $--.--

Trade paper advertisement:

Barrie, J.M. Sentimental Tommy. NY 1896
1st ed. illus. VG $--

or, if space is at a premium:

Barrie. Sentimental Tommy. NY 1st VG $--

* * * * *

APPENDIX

TRADE PAPERS

A number of trade papers circulate
for OP booksellers, of which <u>AB Bookman's Weekly</u> is the largest, oldest,
and most stable. Write or call for
current subscription information. If
you plan to quote heavily to advertising dealers, be sure to pay the
extra for first class delivery.

AB BOOKMAN'S WEEKLY
P.O. Box AB
Clifton, New Jersey 07015

* * * * *

<u>Bookseller</u> is another long-time
publication, issued semi-monthly, that
lists hundreds of books wanted by dealers from all over the country. Circulation isn't as large as AB's, but the
lower subscription and advertising
rates, plus the fact that <u>Bookseller</u>'s
subscribers are dedicated and active
dealers, means this is a good vehicle
for making first contacts and locating
more common books. Write for subscription information and sample copy.

BOOKSELLER
P.O. Box 8183
Ann Arbor, Michigan 48107

* * * * *

Most publications for booksellers
tend to be well-intentioned but short-
lived. A few sophisticated magazines

exist for book collectors, but are too specialized and technical for beginners. A visit to your library is strongly advised.

* * * * *

PRICE GUIDES

Mandeville's Used Book Price Guide is very useful for checking the values of common titles not normally listed in other guides. As a beginner, you'll likely wear this book out. Although spurned by some experienced dealers for its simplicity, the UBPG is a good place to get started.

Mandeville's Used Book Price Guide: Retail Prices of Used, Scarce & Rare Books from U.S. and Canadian Used Book Dealers' Catalogs through December 1988.

```
1989 Edition ............... $89.00
1983 Edition ............... $79.00
1977 Edition ............... $49.00
```

U.S. Funds. Add $5.00 per volume for postage/handling.

PRICE GUIDE PUBLISHERS
P.O. Box 82525
Kenmore, Washington 98028

* * * * *

Bookman's Price Index is the price guide of choice for most booksellers. Few dealers need every volume or can afford them, and the very latest will

be current long after it has paid for
itself. This is the most accurate
indicator of market trends, listing
retail prices of books valued $25.00
and up, as compiled from nearly 200
dealers' catalogs. (Each BPI is around
1,000 pages long.) If your library
doesn't carry this set, put in a
request for it. Otherwise you may have
to come up with the $180 or more per
volume. Write for current information
and a catalog of many reference books
of interest to booksellers.

GALE RESEARCH, INC.
Penobscot Building
Detroit, Michigan 48226

* * * * *

American Book Prices Current is a
valuable wholesale price guide, listing
the prices realized at auction on
better books ($50.00+) sold around the
world. In addition to books, sales
results of maps, charts, serials,
autographs and manuscripts are listed,
along with bibliographic information.
Again, check with your library before
ordering.

Volume 95 (auction year 1989) is available for $81.95 + $4.50 shipping/
handling. The 1983-1987 two-volume
index is $390 + $9.95 shipping/
handling.

AMERICAN BOOK PRICES CURRENT
P.O. Box 236
Washington, Connecticut 06793

* * * * *

When shopping for price guides for your business, avoid the mass-market books you'll find at mall bookshops. Aimed at the layman, such guides tend to inflate values, provide skimpy information, or are so out-of-date as to lack usefulness. The initial investment may seem high, but stick with the professional guides.

* * * * *

REFERENCE BOOKS

The following titles may be available at your local bookstore or library. Read as many as you can <u>before</u> you plunge into the business!

Ahearn, Allen. <u>The Book of First Books</u>
Bonn, Thomas L. <u>Paperback Primer</u>, A Guide for Collectors
Carter, John. <u>A.B.C. for Book Collectors</u>
McBride, Bill. <u>A Pocket Guide to the Identification of First Editions</u>
McBride, Bill. <u>Points of Issue</u>
Rawlins, Ray. <u>The Stein & Day Book of World Autographs</u>
Tannen, Jack. <u>How to Identify and Collect American First Editions</u>
Wilson, Robert A. <u>Modern Book Collecting</u>
Winterich, John T. & David A. Randall. <u>A Primer of Book Collecting</u>

Some of these books, and many others you'll find helpful, are available through The Spoon River Press. They'll be happy to send you a current catalog.

THE SPOON RIVER PRESS
P.O. Box 3676
Peoria, Illinois   61614

* * * * *

Ahearn, Allen. <u>Book Collecting</u>. A
Comprehensive Guide. As well as
providing a general overview of book
collecting, this book also serves as
a value guide to the first books of
over 3,500 collected authors. $19.95

"Author Price Guides" as compiled by
Patricia and Allen Ahearn. (Each
guide includes a facsimile of the
author's signature, a brief bio-
graphical sketch, an up-to-date list
of the author's first American and
British editions, with entries for
limited and trade editions, number of
copies (if available), how to
identify the first edition, and
estimated values. Write for current
list of authors available and
prices.)

QUILL & BRUSH
P.O. Box 5365
Rockville, Maryland   20851

* * * * *

DIRECTORIES

Dealer directories are issued
annually by various publishers, and
you'll need one or two good ones for
establishing your mailing list. The
best ones present dealer/bookstore
names in alphabetical order, geo-

graphical location, and specialty
interest. An old directory is worthless and must be shunned. Two of the
more dependable directories are listed
below. Write for current ordering
information.

BUY BOOKS WHERE - SELL BOOKS WHERE
Ruth E. Robinson
Route 7, Box 162-A
Morgantown, West Virginia   26505

DIRECTORY OF SPECIALIZED
AMERICAN BOOKSELLERS
American Book Collector, Inc.
P.O. Box 867
Ossining, New York   10562

* * * * *

The 1990 Antiquarian Book Fair &
Paper Show Directory (including base-
ball card, comic book, postcard, photograph and print shows for U.S. and
Canada) -- "When & Where & How to Get
There" is now available for $8.50
postpaid (Massachusetts residents add
.45 sales tax) from:

ISAIAH THOMAS BOOKS
980 Main Street
Worcester, Massachusetts   01603

* * * * *

SEARCH SERVICES

Dozens of search services issue long
want lists on a regular basis. Listed

below are a few general OP dealers who
have proven to be dependable contacts.

INTERNATIONAL BOOKFINDERS
P.O. Box 1
Pacific Palisades, California 90272

A POINTS NORTHE
3630 N.W. 22nd
Oklahoma City, Oklahoma 73107

(James Neill Northe also acts as
distributor for some indispensable
reference guides. Write for
more information.)

THE TRACERY BOOKS
P.O. Box 670236
Dallas, Texas 75367-0236

* * * * *

AUCTION HOUSES

   Auction galleries run the gamut of
back-room sellers of box lots to black
tie affairs offering museum-quality
collectors' editions. Catalogs are
available on a yearly subscription
basis, although some companies will
continue to provide catalogs as long as
you participate in their auctions.
Don't balk at the high rates -- catalogs are expensive to produce, and some
become valuable reference materials in
the future.

NEW HAMPSHIRE BOOK AUCTIONS
Woodbury Road
Weare, New Hampshire   03281

Catalogued book, print, map and
ephemera auctions from
May through October
Subscription rate: $15.00
with prices realized
(Canada & overseas, $30.00)

* * * * *

WAVERLY AUCTIONS, INC.
4931 Cordell Avenue, Suite AA
Bethesda, Maryland   20814

Consignment auctions of Fine Books,
Prints, Maps, Autographs & Fine Art
Subscription rate: 8 catalogs
with prices realized: $30.00
Single issue $6.00 first class mail.

* * * * *

PLANDOME BOOK AUCTIONS
P.O. Box 395
Glen Head, New York   11545

Quality books, moderate values.

* * * * *

SAMUEL YUDKIN & ASSOCIATES
1125 King Street
Alexandria, Virginia   22314

General used books, low to
moderate values, plus prints.

* * * * *

ABBREVIATIONS

aeg = all edges gilt
ALs = autograph letter signed (meaning
   a handwritten letter with signature)
BC, BCE or BOMC = book club edition/
   Book-of-the-Month Club
b&w = black & white
bds & cl = boards and cloth (cardboard
   covers with cloth spine)
c = copyright
ca = estimated
cc = copies
CWO = Cash with Order (prepayment
   required)
deco = decorated
dj = dust jacket
dw = dust wrapper
ed = editor or edition
epp = endpaper (paste-down)
epps = both endpapers (paste-down +
   fepp)
ex-lib = ex-library copy
fepp = free endpaper
ffepp = front free epp
foxed = with brown spots and patches
illus = illustrated or illustrator
lea = leather
lt or sl = light or slight (as wear)
ltd = limited (as in "ltd ed")
ND = no publication date noted
NP = no publication place noted
# = "number" (as in #101/500 cc,
   meaning this book is the 101st copy
   out of an edition of 500 copies; be
   aware that "1/500 cc" means that the
   book is one of 500 copies, not
   necessarily numbered.)
obl = oblong, as when a book is bound
   on its short end
o/w = otherwise

pp = pages (p = page)
ppk = paperback
pict = pictorial (as in covers with
  illustrations)
pres = presented or presentation
sgd = signed
teg or gte = top edge gilt/gilt top
  edge
TLs = typed letter signed
w.a.f. = with all faults (sold "as is")
wraps = paper covers, softbound
wr = wear

<u>Cities of publication</u> are frequently
abbreviated, the most common being
"NY."   Also: Phil (Philadelphia),
L (London), Chg (Chicago), B (Boston),
GC (Garden City, NY).

<u>Condition</u>

>   F = Fine
>   VG = Very Good
>   G = Good
>   Fr = Fair
>   P = Poor
>   rc = Reading Copy

<u>Book Sizes</u>

Listed below are American standards for
book sizes, although few dealers are so
exacting. Measurements given in
inches.

>   Atlas folio: 16 x 25
>   Elephant folio: 14 x 23
>   Folio: 12 x 15

```
      Quarto (4to):  9 x 12
            Octavo:  6 x 9
Duodecimo (12mo):  5 x 7.5
             16mo:  4.25 x 6.75
             18mo:  4 x 6.25
             24mo:  3.5 x 6
             32mo:  3.25 x 5
             48mo:  2.5 x 4
             64mo:  2 x 3
```